DATE DUE

3.2.05			
5.9.05			
07/15/09			

Demco No. 62-0549

D0108386

A FALCON GUIDE®

489432

Mountain Biking
Minnesota

Steve Johnson

FALCON®

GUILFORD, CONNECTICUT
HELENA, MONTANA

AN IMPRINT OF THE GLOBE PEQUOT PRESS

For my brother.
WELCOME HOME

_A_FALCONGUIDE ®

All interior photos by Steve Johnson except photo on page 79
Maps by M. A. Dubé

Library of Congress Cataloging-in-Publication Data
Johnson, Steve, 1965–
    Mountain biking Minnesota / Steve Johnson.—1st ed.
        p. cm.—(A Falcon guide)
    ISBN 0-7627-1157-4
    1. All terrain cycling—Minnesota—Guidebooks. 2. Bicycle trails—Minnesota—Guidebooks. 3. Minnesota—Guidebooks. I. Title. II. Series

GV1045.5.M55 J65 2002
917.7604'54—dc21

Manufactured in the United States of America
First Edition/First Printing

Contents

Acknowledgments

My words here will never seem adequate to express my appreciation for all the support I had during this project. I got to spend two full seasons exploring nearly 1,000 miles of trails all over our great state, but in the chaotic early stages of this project to do that solo while working a seven-day-a-week job was brutal. Thanks also go to Erin Turner and staff at Globe Pequot for helping finish it off.

I'd be nowhere without my family. My recurring plea to them for two years was, "Can you cover for me? I have to leave town for three days." And they were always there for me. Dad, thanks for running the show. You're the best.

Peggy O'Neill McLeod at Falcon was the greatest. You are about to read a better book because of her expert tutelage. Thank you, Peggy!

Steve Simmer and Ron Hains at the Minnesota Department of Natural Resources pointed me in the right direction and provided contact throughout the state. With their help, and additional hints from park and forest staff all over Minnesota, I was able to find the best trails out there.

My experience at Lutsen was one of the highlights of my final summer of riding, thanks to Jim Vick, head mountain biking honcho. He is a big reason why Lutsen boasts some of the most bitchin' trails in the country.

Tucked away off the road and behind some trees in Grand Marais, you might (or might not) find Mark Spinler in his Superior North Outdoor Center. I was there only briefly but felt like an old friend. Mark is the Jeremiah Johnson of the North Country, wandering the woods in search of another place to ride—or maybe just wandering the woods. He can show you every bike trail, hiking trail, logging road, and deer path in all the land. Thanks, Mark, for the hints and a new perspective on mountain biking.

Thanks to John Filander at Giants Ridge for all the enthusiasm and extra help with his trails. John likes people to think that he's putting in a tough day at the office, but we're not fooled. It can't be all bad to have to go out and "check on the condition of the trails" day after day. The trails at The Ridge are top-notch because of John's hard work and excitement for the sport.

My buddy Doug, who always seems to win races without training, stoked my competitive fire way back in 1987. From now on, we ride for Bob.

Most of all, my wife deserves the special thanks that I can't properly bestow. I deserted you on many a summer weekend to toil on the trails, and I enjoyed too many gorgeous views and quiet sunsets without you. Next year I hope you'll come along. We've got a groovy kind of love.

Preface

And the end of all our exploring
will be to arrive where we started
and know the place for the first time.
                    —Unknown

It was on one of the last trails where it finally happened. I floated along several miles of narrow singletrack on a velvety carpet of fallen autumn leaves when the scene abruptly changed. The trail emerged onto a smooth rock mountaintop, decorated with dwarf pines backlit by an early morning sun. Beyond was the magnificent expanse of Lake Superior, and while I gazed slack-jawed at all of that beauty, my front wheel slipped into a crack in the rock and I clumsily crashed. It wasn't even a crash worth bragging about. I could have at least scraped off a little skin.

The day of the crash I was pedaling along the transcendent North Shore of Lake Superior, along rugged rock formations and in primeval woodlands. A week later I enjoyed intimate forest roads braided through towering stands of virgin pine (and experienced the ghostly howls of a large pack of timber wolves). I played on grassy ski trails hidden in stands of birch and aspen and spruce. In the heart of the city I explored wooded river valleys on trails rim-deep with sand, open prairie riding in regional parks, and steep climbing at ski areas. Farther south, rolling bluffland provided trails through veritable rock fields, along hard-packed dirt paths in dense hardwood forests, and past cornfields.

Minnesota offers a rich diversity of landscape that makes for endless fun on a mountain bike. Retreating glaciers did all the work for us, leaving behind the hills and dales common in the southern part of the state and the mystical lands of the North Country. As I labored in my work compiling the trails for this book, I discovered areas I had never visited and came back to some I had last seen as a small boy. I've lived here my whole life, but I was consistently amazed each time I turned my pedals through the distinct natural regions that make up our state. Some were familiar, like Gooseberry, Jay Cooke, and Split Rock. Others, like Pincushion Mountain, the southeast bluffland, and the big national forests up north, were brand new.

I attempted to include rides in this book that everyone can enjoy. I think these are some of the best that Minnesota has to offer, and rookies to experts will find plenty of fat tire miles to choose from. I rode along with a couple of sprites on pint-sized bikes on the flat Mendota Trail and followed two energetic young brothers up the gnarly climbs at Holzinger Lodge. Intermediate riders can pick almost anywhere in the state and find a favorite trail. Try Cherry Hill in Winona for a rolling ride and breath-taking views of the river valley. Maybe the maze of wooded paths and long climbs at Battle Creek will spin your wheels. Or flawless singletrack in the Sawtooths at Lutsen, with the mighty Lake Superior for a backdrop. Visitors will return for the epic environs, and locals have a lifetime of trails at their disposal.

There's a catch to this, however. There are so many other great things to do, you might get distracted from your bike. Camping in the North Country is tough to beat. There are hundreds of campgrounds scattered about, and even more backcountry sites for the hardy crowd. On some of the fun mountain bike routes, you will cross several hiking trails that offer another diversion. Two of them are real beauties and are sure to have you coming back for more. The Superior Hiking Trail, from Duluth to Grand Marais, is one of the best in the nation. Just take a few steps and you'll agree. The North Country Trail is an event in itself. Take a whole season and follow it from North Dakota to upstate New York. Some of the trail's most memorable miles can be found right here in Minnesota. And with all the lakes we've got, water sports are a big draw. Fishing in the northland is world class, and water skiing, swimming, and tubing are popular. If you like to canoe, look no further. Paddling the Boundary Waters is an experience you won't get anywhere else on the planet. You might come with the intention of riding your bike, but all the side trips may be too hard to resist.

You might notice the absence of mountain biking as a recreation choice in many park and forest brochures. Our sport has a tenuous relationship with other outdoor groups, partly because of perceived environmental damage, and partly from ill-fated encounters on the trail. The former concern is a valid one, if responsible riding practices are not observed. Let's face it, our fat, bumpy tires are going to affect the ground more than, say, a hiking boot. But the problems arise when those tires pound through a muddy trail, or skid down a hill, or careen around a turn and send chunks of earth sailing into the stratosphere. If the trail falls into disrepair, it will eventually be closed, and that's just no good at all. A more significant issue—but one with an easy solution—is negative trail encounters with other users. Outdoor recreation is a big deal for a lot of folks in Minnesota, and you're bound to meet someone else while you're out riding. A favorite trail in the metro area is in grave danger of being shut down to bikes because a few lunatics can't (or won't) control their speed and riding habits. Ride with respect for others, yield first, stop and say hi. The best trails are open trails.

That said, I hope you enjoy reading and using this book as much as I did writing it. I'm glad I had the opportunity to share my experiences with you. Grab your bike, find a trail, and head to the woods. Bring a friend. Bring a child, one of yours or borrow one. Bring a spouse (you could borrow one of those, too, I suppose).

My job here is finished. The book is done. I'm going ridin'! Hope to see you on the trails.

Map Legend

Interstate		Waterway/Waterfall	
U.S. Highway		Lake/Reservoir	
State or Other Principal Road		Meadow/Swamp	
Forest Road		Building/Hut	
Interstate Highway		Gate	
Paved Road		Parking Area	
Gravel Road		Bridge	
Unimproved Road (doubletrack)		Wilderness Boundary	
Trail (singletrack)		Map Orientation	
Trail Marker		Scale	

0   0.5   1

MILES

Ride Locations

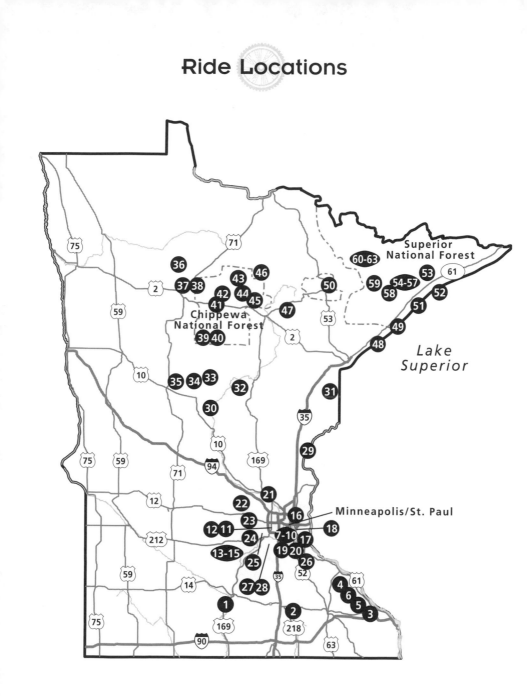

Introduction

I stared blankly at my map for a half hour again this morning trying to discover a worthy route I could turn the pedals on. This is a familiar scene for many mountain bikers. Those who live in an urban area have limited choices to begin with, and even the folks living way out there might like to learn of a new route to sample.

If you're new to the area, where can you go to ride? Where can you even look to locate a trail? If you are a long-time local, how do you avoid the customary pilgrimage to the same old trails week after week? If only there were a way to find new and challenging terrain and areas that are fat tire friendly. Or to find a place to just roll along and enjoy the sights when you're not in the mood for a hammerfest.

Welcome to *Mountain Biking Minnesota.* Here are sixty-three rides ranging from easy spins on a flat park path, to smooth singletracks, to steep, rock-strewn hills and remote forest roads. This book will take you from the rolling river bluffs in the southeastern part of the state to the hidden trails in the big cities and up north to the rugged cliffs and deep woods of our national forests. The rides are described in plain language, with accurate distances and ratings for physical and technical difficulty. Each entry offers a wealth of detailed information that's easy to read and use, from your couch or on the trail. Our aim is threefold: to help you choose a ride that's appropriate for your fitness and skill level; to make it easy to find the trailhead; and to help you complete the ride in one piece, without getting lost. Take care of these basics and big fun is bound to break loose.

About Minnesota

I picked up a client from the airport recently, and he voiced his amazement as we drove through the Minnesota River Valley. "I thought Minnesota was one big glacier," he said. Nope, no glaciers here anymore. It feels like it sometimes, but most of the year this is a mighty fine place to live. Spring bursts from winter's grasp and cloaks the state with a dozen shades of green. Summer days are hot with humidity that steams right through your very soul, and fall lingers with beaming colors and cool breezes. Sure, winter can hang around for six months, but hard weather makes us proud folks. Before we talk bikes, I'll throw a little background information at you. Even I didn't know some of this stuff.

Minnesota's name is derived from a Sioux word that means "land of cloudy water." The water in question is the Minnesota River, which really is kind of murky. But people are most familiar with our state's nickname, Land of 10,000 Lakes. That sounds like lotsa lakes, but there are actually more than 15,000! No shortage of water here. You may also hear Minnesota called the Gopher State or the North Star State (*L'Etoile du Nord,* if you're feeling kind of French).

WHAT DOES MINNESOTA LOOK LIKE?

There are several major natural regions of the United States, and Minnesota has parts of two of them: the Superior Upland (Canadian Shield) and the Central Lowland. Much of the Superior Upland is fashioned with low, rounded hills covered in places with mantle rock. The movement of glaciers created basins in the rock that have become some of our many lakes. In addition to lakes, Minnesota is home to many swamp and wetland areas and large peat bogs in the north. The northern area of the state also contains numerous shallow streams and narrow rivers that cascade over falls and through deep gorges. There are even mountains up there! Yep, the Sawtooth Mountains, some of the oldest in the world, rise in rolling fashion just west of Lake Superior. The highest point in the state is in this area: 2,301-foot Eagle Mountain. Altitude sickness probably won't get to you, but these hills will still test your limits.

The Central Lowland sections of Minnesota vary significantly. In the northwest reside the largest peat bogs in the lower forty-eight states, on what was once glacial Lake Agassiz. The southwest contains prairie hills and till left from old glacial advances and rich, fertile soil (much of our agriculture thrives in the southern half of Minnesota). The southeast boasts an unglaciated area with exciting rolling bluffs and deep valleys. The Mississippi River borders this scenic region to the east.

WATER EVERYWHERE!

Flying over Minnesota is the best way to get a feel for just how much water is out there. The 10,000 lakes that get all the bragging rights are just those that are large enough to be called a lake; there are probably the same number of smaller lakes and ponds, as well as many wetland areas. Several of our lakes are biggies, like Leech and Mille Lacs and Winnibigoshish. Of course, the granddaddy of them all is Lake Superior, but the term "lake" is hardly a suitable title. Call it an inland sea, the largest of its kind on the planet; it's colder and deeper and meaner than all the rest. It's moody, too. I've gazed from the North Shore over calm, twinkling waters nearly 100 miles to the Apostle Islands, and I've braced myself against a fierce Nor'easter while huge breakers angrily pounded the shore, scattering tree-sized hunks of driftwood like so many broken matchsticks. Superior is alive, and its spirit is what so many of us have come to embrace.

Three major watersheds drain Minnesota. Lands north and west of Lake Superior empty through smaller streams directly into the big lake or into the St. Louis River. Lake Superior's waters flow to the St. Lawrence River and then to the Atlantic Ocean. Water in a second watershed drains the majority of the northern portions of the state into Rainy River and Lake of the Woods, where it continues across the Canadian border to the Nelson

River and then on to Hudson Bay. The rest of Minnesota is drained by the mighty Mississippi River, which begins its long journey to the Gulf of Mexico at Lake Itasca. Ol' Miss has help from the St. Croix River on the eastern border and from the Minnesota River, which begins way over at the western edge of the state and wanders all the way across to its confluence with the Mississippi just west of downtown St. Paul.

IT'S SO GREEN!

We are fortunate here in Minnesota to have regular rainfall that gives rise to an ample supply of foliage. Although there is only a ridiculously small percentage (about 1 percent) of the majestic red and white pine forests that once covered the state, the current birch, poplar, and maple stands, mixed with remaining pine, still make for an impressive sight. The lower two-thirds of the state comprise broadleaf deciduous forests of oak, maple, elm, and basswood, particularly in the far southeastern corner. Much of the southern and western areas of Minnesota are used for agriculture and were cleared for that use long ago. There also once was a vast tallgrass prairie in the south and west, but now less than 1 percent of that remains.

THE WILD LIFE

Minnesota has an abundance of wildlife of many types. The northern areas are home to black bear, moose, white-tailed deer (found statewide), and the largest timber wolf population in the lower forty-eight. In addition to the big guys, you might also spot beaver, woodchuck, fox, and coyotes, or pine marten, weasel, and river otter. Gophers and squirrels are also very common. Closer to the ground are leopard frogs, toads, salamanders, snakes, and turtles. The hardwood forests are favorite haunts of grouse and wild turkey. Also look for ducks, loons, swans, geese, and herons. The bald eagle and several species of hawk and owl grace the skies, and there are lots of fish! Muskie, walleye, trout, and sunfish are prevalent.

PEOPLE AND PLACES

Oh ya sure, you betcha, doncha know! Cripes, you'd tink da folk in Minnesoota talk funny, or sometin'. Yes, we have lots of Norwegians, Swedes, and Germans here in Minnesota. There is also influence from Finland, Poland, and Czechoslovakia. Aye, and we're a hardy breed, recreating with verve in all seasons. Minnesota's outdoors are the stuff of legend. Camping, canoeing, hunting, and fishing are very popular, especially in the huge Boundary Waters Canoe Area and Voyageurs National Park. People don't stay inside in the winter, either. Skiing, skating, snowmobiling, hockey, and ice fishing are some of the mainstays of our free time. Two national forests, Superior and Chippewa, and nearly eighty state parks provide over five million acres of outdoor playground.

That depends on your dedication and/or sanity. Minnesota's weather spans a wide range of extremes. Snow has been known to linger into May, and 40 inches piled up in October recently. It is possible to get some riding in during the winter; however, keep in mind that Minneapolis is the coldest major city on the planet, and don't be surprised to see the mercury drop to minus 50! There also tend to be several ice storms every winter, and that's just plain ugly. (Stay inside with a good book and a warm fire.) They say the average winter temperature is 14°F in the southern half of the state and –18°F in the north, but it can stray well away from those numbers. Bitter wind chills are common, sending the "coldness factor" plummeting to 70, 80, and even 90 below! Summer highs can climb above 100 degrees and be laced with stifling humidity. July temps hover around 75 in the south and 60 up north, perfect for pedaling. Spring is usually wet (muddy) with varying temperatures and is a difficult time to ride; the northern trails stay wetter longer. Fall is cool and comfortable with dry conditions and is typically the best season for bikes.

Riding conditions are usually at their finest from early June to mid-October. Spring weather or heavy summer rains may make parts or all of some trails unrideable. Keep in mind that some hunting seasons may also overlap the riding season. If you're riding in an area with bullets flying, don't wear your moose antler bike helmet. Wear blaze orange and check with the Department of Natural Resources for specific hunting dates (see Appendix B).

Riding in Minnesota: What to Expect

The rides in this book cover a wide variety of terrain. Many of the routes begin innocently enough on pavement or smooth gravel, then change to steep, rutted paths littered with rocks. We have quite a selection of trail types throughout the state. Rolling hills and bluff country grace the southeast, with hard-packed dirt and gravel singletrack. The metro area offers more fun dirt trails and some well-maintained cross-country ski loops. The lush valley trails along the Minnesota and Mississippi rivers are some favorites, and many of the local and county parks have done an excellent job including mountain bikes. Traveling north, the riding gets even better. Singletrack trails to primitive logging trails and scenic forest roads are all at your disposal. Numerous state parks and two national forests provide riders with thousands of miles of fun. Many of these routes travel through some of the most magnificent landscapes in the country.

Certain details of your preparations for an easy spin on a flat forest road will be quite a bit different than for an extended tour deep into the woods. On some rides, the terrain can change drastically from one mile to the next. It is important to be ready for those changes before setting out. Put in plenty of miles on your bike to get in good shape ahead of time, and know your limits. Clean your bike's rims, brakes, handlebars, seat, shifters, derailleurs, and chain to make sure they survived the last trip and are functioning properly. Get into this habit after your ride, also. There's a lot of mud on many of the low-lying routes here, and your bike will thank you if you clean the goop off before it ruins bearings, cogs, and other important parts.

A helmet is essential for mountain biking: It can save your life and prevent serious injuries. My face landed on a log one day, and thanks to my helmet I left the scene with only a big knot on my head. Don't ride without a helmet. Cycling gloves are another indispensable piece of safety equipment that can save hands from cuts and bruises from falls, encroaching branches, and rocks. They also improve your grip and comfort on the handlebars.

Always pack or carry at least one full water bottle. On longer rides, don't leave the house without two or three bottles or one of the handy hydration packs, or plan your ride so it passes someplace where potable water is available. A snack such as fruit or energy bars can keep those huge quads cranking for extra hours and prevent the dreaded "bonk": the sudden loss of energy when your body runs out fuel. Dress for the weather, and pack a jacket that repels both wind and water in case the weather turns ugly. Don't forget sunglasses, sunscreen (use the sports stuff that won't run down into your eyes and mouth), lip balm, and insect repellant, which is especially critical for mid-summer riding.

A basic tool kit can save you from a long walk or even a dark night out in the woods. A tire pump and tube patch kit are vital, and a few other tools can make the difference between disaster and a five-minute pit stop. Carry a set of allen wrenches or an all-in-one tool for tightening or adjusting seat post, handlebars, chainrings, pedals, brake posts, and other components. I generally carry just a minimum, but some folks aren't comfortable unless they bring a whole shop's worth of tools. They're weighted down, and wrenches rattle with every bump in the trail, but those riders are rarely stranded by mechanical failures.

This book was written to provide an overview of the wide variety of rides here in Minnesota. The maps and ride descriptions presented here provide sufficient information to reach the trails and ride them without getting lost. USGS topographic maps can provide a more detailed view of the terrain, but most ride routes in this book are not shown; only the northern forest roads and some major trails will appear. I have listed some of the clearest and most attainable maps for each ride, including a USGS quad and available park brochures. Use the one that works best for you, but be sure to include some form of map with your on-trail gear, especially if you are unfamiliar with the area. Combine park brochures or local trail maps with the detailed descriptions in this book for a worry-free ride.

IMBA Rules of the Trail

I can hear you grumbling. "Oh, great," you're thinking. "Here's another yahoo telling us how we should ride." Relax. The rules of the trail are merely reminders to all riders that taking care of the trails and being courteous to your fellow trail users helps to keep our favorite rides open and in great shape. If every mountain biker always yielded the right-of-way, stayed on the trail, avoided wet or muddy trails, never cut through a meadow, showed respect for other trail users, and carried out every last scrap of what he or she carried in (energy bar wrappers, destroyed tubes, etc.)—we wouldn't need a list of rules governing our sport.

Fact is, most mountain bikers are conscientious and are trying to do the right thing. (No one becomes good at something as demanding and painful as grunting up steep ridges by cheating.) Most of us don't need rules. But we do need knowledge of what exactly is the right thing to do.

Here are some guidelines (friendly reminders), reprinted by permission from the International Mountain Bicycling Association, with a comment or two of my own. The basic idea is to prevent or avoid conflicts with other backcountry visitors and users. Do your part to maintain trail access by observing the following rules of the trail. IMBA's mission is to promote environmentally sound and socially responsible mountain biking.

1. **Ride on open trails only.** Respect trail and road closures (ask if not sure); avoid possibly trespassing on private land; obtain permits and authorization as may be required. Federal and state wilderness areas are closed to cycling. The way you ride will influence trail management decisions and policies.

2. **Leave no trace.** Be sensitive to the dirt beneath you. Even on open (legal) trails, you should not ride under conditions where you will leave evidence of your passing, such as on certain soils after a rain. Recognize different types of soil and trail construction; practice low-impact cycling. (Ride softly and carry a big . . . pump.) This also means staying on existing trails and not creating new ones. Be sure to pack out at least as much as you pack in.

3. **Control your bicycle!** Inattention for even a second can cause problems. Obey all bicycle speed regulations and recommendations.

4. **Always yield trail.** Make known your approach well in advance. A friendly greeting (or bell) is considerate and works well; don't startle others. Show your respect when passing by slowing to a walking pace or stopping. Anticipate other trail users at corners and blind spots.

5. **Never spook animals.** All animals are startled by an unannounced approach, a sudden movement, or a loud noise. This can be dangerous for you, others, and the animals. Give animals extra room and time to

adjust to you. When passing horses use special care and follow directions from the horseback riders (dismount and ask if uncertain). Running cattle and disturbing wildlife is a serious offense. Leave gates as you found them or as marked.

6. **Plan ahead.** Know your equipment, your ability, and the area in which you are riding and prepare accordingly. Be self-sufficient at all times, keeping your equipment in good repair, and carrying the necessary supplies for changes in weather or other conditions. A well-executed trip is a satisfaction to you and not a burden or offense to others. Always wear a helmet.

Keep trails open by setting a good example of environmentally sound and socially responsible off-road cycling. Following are some poignant thoughts from Gary Sjoquist, mountain bike advocate and co-founder of Minnesota Off-Road Cyclists.

GAINING AND MAINTAINING MOUNTAIN BIKE TRAILS

If you swing a leg over a mountain bike to go for a ride, you'll have checked to see if there's air in your tires, a helmet on your head, gloves on your hands, and water in your bottle. You'll also have picked a trail to ride on—maybe it's your favorite section of singletrack or an old logging road. We do these things as part of the routine; it's what we do beforehand so we'll have an enjoyable experience out on the trail.

Unlike road bicycling, however, where you're legally entitled a place to ride, mountain bikers can only ride on trails that someone or some group has fought for or negotiated to use. Whether it's an old logging road, a cross-country ski trail, or gnarly singletrack, advocates were involved in getting mountain bike use approved, the trail designed and built, and then maintained. But if nobody negotiates for mountain bike use, or helps design, build, and maintain the trails, there won't be trails to ride on.

As a mountain biker, please do your part—get involved in gaining and maintaining trails so we'll have cool places to ride in the future. Join the International Mountain Bicycling Association (IMBA) and support their fight for our right to ride at the national level. Then join a local, statewide, or regional advocacy group and get involved at whatever level you can: attending meetings, helping with trail maintenance sessions, or as part of the leadership of the organization.

Like helmets, gloves, and water bottles, the process of gaining and maintaining trails is part of the mountain biking routine: It's what we all have to do to ensure that we can keep riding. If we don't do it, who will?

Gary Sjoquist
MN Representative, International Mountain Bicycling Association
Co-Founder, Minnesota Off-Road Cyclists

How to Use This Guide

Mountain Biking Minnesota describes sixty-three mountain bike rides in their entirety. Some additional routes in the area are mentioned briefly in Appendix A. Many of the featured rides are loops, beginning and ending at the same point. Loops are by far the most popular type of ride, and this book has bunches of 'em. Other rides are the out-and-back flavor, and some just wander around.

Be forewarned, however: The difficulty of a loop ride may change dramatically depending on which direction you ride around the loop. If you are unfamiliar with the rides in this book, try them first as described here. The directions follow the path of least resistance (which does not necessarily mean easy). After you've been over the terrain, you can determine whether a given loop would be fun—or even imaginable—in the reverse direction.

Portions of some rides follow gravel or paved roads; others never even see a road. Purists may wince at rides on paved roads or bike paths in a book about mountain biking, but these are special rides. They offer a chance to enjoy the forest and fresh air while covering easier, nontechnical terrain for people new to the sport. They can also be used by hard-core riders on "active rest" days or when other trails are closed or too wet.

Each ride description in this book follows the same format:

Number and name of the ride: Rides are cross-referenced by number throughout this book. In many cases, parts of rides or entire routes can be linked to other rides for longer trips or variations on a standard route. These opportunities are noted. For some of the names of rides I relied on official names of trails, roads, and natural features as shown on U.S. Geological Survey and park maps. Some of them I created based on my own rides. In some cases, signs or trail markers in the field may show slightly different names.

Location: The general whereabouts of the ride; distance and directions from the nearest town.

Distance: The length of the ride in miles, given as a loop, one way, or round trip.

Time: An estimate of how long it takes to complete the ride, for example: 1 to 2 hours. *The time listed is the actual riding time and does not include rest stops.* Strong, skilled riders may be able to do a given ride in less than the estimated time; other riders may take considerably longer. Bear in mind that severe weather, changes in trail conditions, or mechanical problems may prolong a ride.

Tread: The type of road or trail: paved road, gravel road, doubletrack, or singletrack.

Aerobic level: The level of physical effort required to complete the ride: easy, moderate, or strenuous. (See explanation of the rating system on page 10.)

Technical difficulty: The level of bike handling skills needed to complete the ride upright and in one piece. Technical difficulty is rated on a scale from 1 to 5, with 1 being the easiest and 5 the hardest (see the explanation of the rating systems on page 11).

Hazards: A list of dangers that may be encountered on a ride, including traffic, weather, trail obstacles and conditions, risky stream crossings, obscure trails, and other perils. Remember that conditions may change at any time. Be alert for storms, new fences, downfalls, missing trail signs, and mechanical failures. Fatigue, heat, cold, and/or dehydration may impair judgment. Always wear a helmet and other safety equipment. Ride in control at all times.

Highlights: Special features or qualities that make a ride worth doing (as if we needed an excuse!), such as scenery, fun singletrack, and chances to see widlife.

Land status: A list of managing agencies or land owners. Many of the rides in this book travel on state and national lands, but some also cross portions of private, county, or municipal lands. Do not enter areas where riding isn't allowed, and respect the land regardless of who owns it. See Appendix B for a list of local addresses for land management agencies. **Stay on the trail or stay home.**

Maps: A list of available maps. A good state map or the *Minnesota Gazetteer* will provide a decent overview of the state and show some elevation intervals. USGS topographic maps in the *7.5-Minute Quad Series* provide a close-up look at terrain, but few of the rides are shown. Not all routes are shown on official maps; in fact, some of the rides follow unmapped routes. Beware the urge to ride on every spur trail you see, as many will lead to dead ends or onto private land.

Access: How to find the trailhead or start of the ride. A number of rides begin right from a town; for others it's best to drive to an outlying trailhead.

Notes on the trail: A bonus section outlining personal thoughts and extra details on the ride. I'll relate my grumblings or accolades about a certain trail or an interesting experience when I was out there. Other times there will just be a closer look at what to expect out on the trail.

The ride: A mile-by-mile list of key points—landmarks, notable climbs and descents, stream crossings, obstacles, hazards, major turns and junctions—along the ride. All distances were measured to the tenth of a mile with a cyclo-computer (a bike-mounted odometer). Terrain, riding technique, and even tire pressure can affect odometer readings, so treat all mileages as estimates.

Finally, one last reminder that the real world is changing all the time. The information presented here is as accurate and up-to-date as possible, but there are no guarantees out in the woods. Chances are fairly good that on some trails you will encounter something that is different than what you've read in this book. Significant changes could occur just in the short time between when I penned my last word and the book's publication. You alone are responsible for your safety and for the choices you make on the trail. Local land management agencies or bike shops can often provide current information.

If you do find an error or omission in this book, or a new and note-worthy change in the field, I'd like to hear from you. Please write to Steve Johnson, c/o Globe Pequot Press, P.O. Box 480, Guilford, CT 06437.

Rating the Rides: One Person's Pain Is Another's Pleasure

One of the first lessons learned by most mountain bikers is not to trust their friends' accounts of how easy or difficult a given ride may be.

"Where ya wanna ride today?"

"Let's just go easy, maybe cruise the valley or somethin'. I've hardly been on the bike at all, don't feel too strong."

If you don't read between the lines, only painful experience will tell you that your buddy eats intervals for breakfast and hammers five-hour training rides "just to get the heart rate up." So how do you know what you're getting into, before it's too late?

Don't always listen to your friends, especially right at the start of a ride. But do read this book. Falcon guides rate each ride for two types of difficulty: the physical effort required to pedal the distance, and the level of bike-handling skills needed to stay vertical and make it home in one piece. We call these *aerobic level* and *technical difficulty*.

The following sections explain what the various ratings mean in plain, specific language and weigh other factors such as elevation gain, total trip distance, weather, wind, and current trail conditions.

AEROBIC LEVEL RATINGS

Bicycling is often touted as a relaxing, low-impact, relatively easy way to burn excess calories and maintain a healthy heart and lungs. Mountain biking, however, tends to pack a little more work (and excitement) into the routine.

Fat tires and soft or rough trails increase the rolling resistance, so it takes more effort to push those wheels around. Unpaved and off-road hills are often steeper than grades measured and tarred by the highway department. When we use the word *steep*, we mean a sweat-inducing, oxygen-sucking, lactose-building climb. If it's followed by an exclamation point—steep!—expect some real pain on the way up (and maybe for days afterward).

Expect to breathe hard and sweat some, probably a lot. Pedaling around town is a good start, but it won't fully prepare you for the workout offered by most of the rides in this book. If you're unsure of your level of fitness, see a doctor for a physical exam before tackling any of these rides. If you're riding to get back in shape or just for the fun of it, take it easy. Walk or rest if need be. Start with short rides and add miles gradually.

Here's how we rate the exertion level for terrain covered in this book:

Easy: Flat or gently rolling terrain. No steep or prolonged climbs.

Moderate: Some hills. Climbs may be short and fairly steep or long and gradual.

Strenuous: Frequent or prolonged climbs steep enough to require riding in the lowest gear; requires a high level of aerobic fitness, power, endurance, and grunting (all typically acquired through many hours of riding and proper training). Less fit riders may need to walk.

Many rides are mostly easy or moderate but may have short strenuous sections. Other rides are mostly strenuous and should be attempted only after a complete medical checkup and implant of a second heart, preferably a *big* one. Also be aware that flailing through a highly technical section can be exhausting even on the flats. Good riding skills and a relaxed stance on the bike save energy.

Finally, any ride can be strenuous if you ride it hard and fast. Conversely, the pain of a lung-burning climb grows easier to tolerate as your fitness level improves. Learn to pace yourself and remember to schedule easy rides and rest days into your calendar.

TECHNICAL DIFFICULTY RATINGS

While you're pushing up that steep, rocky slope, wondering how much farther you can go before your lungs explode and billow out of your mouth like an air bag in a desperate gasp for oxygen, remember that the dry heaves aren't the only hurdle on the way to the top of the hill.

There's that tree across the trail, or the sideslope littered with marble-sized pebbles, or the place where the trail disappears except for tiny pieces of Lycra clinging to the outstretched limbs of a thieving oak tree.

Mountain bikes will roll over or through an amazing array of little challenges. Sometimes we have to help, or at least close our eyes and hang on. Some riders get off their bikes and walk—get this—*before* they flip over the handlebars. These folks have no sense of adventure.

The rest of us hop onto our bikes with only the dimmest inkling of what lies ahead. Later we brag about the Ride to Hell (leaving out the part about carrying our bikes over much of that hellish terrain).

No more. The technical difficulty ratings in this book help take the worst surprises out of backcountry rides. In the privacy of your own home you can make an honest appraisal of your bike-handling skills and then find rides in these pages that match your ability.

I rate technical difficulty on a scale from 1 to 5 (1 being easiest). I tried to make the ratings as objective as possible by considering the type and frequency of the ride's obstacles. The same standards were applied consistently through all the rides in the book. I've also added plus (+) and minus (-) symbols to cover gray areas between given levels of difficulty: a 4+ obstacle is harder than a 4, but easier than a -5. A stretch of trail rated as 5+ would be nearly unrideable by all but the most skilled (or luckiest) riders.

Here are the five levels defined:

Level 1: Smooth tread; road or doubletrack; no obstacles, ruts, or steeps. Requires basic bike riding skills.

Level 2: Mostly smooth tread; wide, well-groomed singletrack or road/ doubletrack with minor ruts or loose gravel or sand.

Level 3: Irregular tread with some rough sections; single or doubletrack with obvious route choices; some steep sections; occasional obstacles may include small rocks, roots, water bars, ruts, loose gravel or sand, and sharp turns.

Level 4: Rough tread with few smooth places; singletrack or rough doubletrack with limited route choices; steep sections, some with obstacles; obstacles are numerous and varied, including rocks, roots, branches, ruts, sidehills, narrow tread, loose gravel or sand, and sharp turns.

Level 5: Continuously broken, rocky, root-infested, or trenched tread; singletrack or extremely rough doubletrack with few route choices; frequent, sudden, and severe changes in gradient; some slopes so steep that wheels lift off the ground; obstacles are nearly continuous and may include boulders, logs, water, large holes, deep ruts, ledges piles of loose gravel, steep sidehills, encroaching trees, and really sharp turns. (Sounds kinda fun, doesn't it?)

Again, most of the rides in this book cover varied terrain, with an ever-changing degree of difficulty. Some trails run smooth with only occasional obstacles; others are seemingly all one big obstacle. The path of least resistance, or *line*, is where you find it. In general, most obstacles are more challenging if you encounter them while climbing than while descending. On the other hand, in heavy surf (e.g., long sections of boulders, tangles of downfall, and deep sand), fear is more common when facing downhill.

Realize, too, that different riders have different strengths and weaknesses. Some folks can scramble over logs and boulders without a grunt, but they crash head-over-sprocket at every sharp, sandy turn. Some fly off the steepest drops; others freeze. Some riders climb like the wind and others just blow . . . and walk.

The key to overcoming "technical difficulties" is practice: keep trying. Follow a rider who makes it look easy and don't hesitate to ask for constructive criticism. Try shifting your weight (good riders move a lot, front to back, side to side, and up and down) and experimenting with balance and momentum. Find a smooth patch of lawn and practice riding as slowly as possible, even balancing at a standstill in a "track stand" (described in the Glossary in the back of this book). This will give you more confidence, and more time to recover or bail out, the next time the trail rears up and bites. See the Glossary for explanations of technical mountain biking terms.

Mount Kato Ski Area

Location: At the outskirts of Mankato; 2 miles south of U.S. Highway 169 on MN Highway 66.
Distance: 4.5-mile loop.
Time: 35–50 minutes.
Tread: Hard-packed singletrack with some grassy doubletrack.
Aerobic level: Moderate.
Technical difficulty: Levels 2 to 4.
Hazards: Loose gravel; steep, sharp turns on some descents.
Highlights: Excellent singletrack riding through thick woods; plenty of challenging climbs and exhilarating downhills.
Land status: Private: Mt. Kato Ski and Bike.
Maps: USGS Mankato West; maps at rental office.
Access: From US 169 in Mankato, go south on MN 66 approximately 2 miles. Mount Kato Ski and Bike Complex will be on your left. Obtain trail pass ($6) from the rental office facing the ski hill.

Notes on the trail: Mount Kato offers a taste of higher country here in our mountain-deficient state. Superb singletrack riding awaits at this young mountain bike park. Opened for fat tires in 1996, Mt. Kato offers nearly 5 miles of fun on its main loop alone, with several offshoot trails for a potential 8 miles of riding and many more if you stay up and explore different loops. Eighty percent of the mileage is on hard-packed wooded singletrack—a dream come true. Riders of all abilities can enjoy these trails, but the terrain of the place requires some extra huffing. Brand new riders might want to get some miles in before tackling Kato. Bikes and helmets are both available for rent if you lack equipment.

The trail starts right off with a respectable climb, switchbacking up toward the top of the hill. Expect some loose gravel and tight switchbacks. Hard-packed dirt prevails on the trail the rest of the way. Some nice views of the surrounding valleys reward your efforts as the trail snakes around a few small ponds on the back side of the main ski runs. Stay on the lookout for deer and fox and stop to hear the frogs and toads chattering at Frog

Mount Kato Ski Area

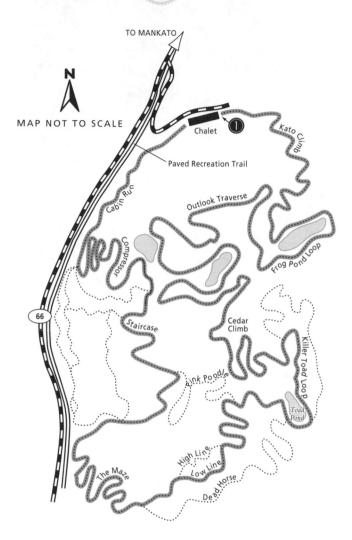

Pond. The trip up Cedar Climb is one of the best I've ridden, with challenging riding and beauteous scenery. Seven trails with the "Most Difficult" label lurk throughout for those with a healthier appetite for danger. Pound for pound, Mt. Kato serves up some of the most technical riding in the state. The main loop drops back to lower elevations on grassy trails through The Maze, then back up Staircase to the top again. A fun descent on Compressor will test your bike-handling skills with a series of twists and turns and sharp switchbacks before depositing you back at the chalet at the base of the mountain.

Coming down the hill at Mount Kato Ski Area.

The Ride

0.0   With your newly acquired trail pass, follow the trail from the chalet on its winding way up Kato Climb (east) to the top of the hill. Circle around Frog Pond and back across Outlook Traverse with long-distance views.

1.3   Trail splits here. Follow the section of trail labeled MORE DIFFICULT, which descends through thick hardwood forest of oak, maple, and aspen. The trail immediately begins to head back uphill on Cedar Climb. This is a fun part of the trail that winds through dense cedar stands on the back side of the mountain. At the top of the climb the trail splits again, giving you the chance to take on the Mad Squirrel expert section. This loop continues on Killer Toad Loop.

2.2   Junction with Dead Horse expert trail near Toad Pond. Go right on your present course toward Low Line.

2.4   Another junction with a chance to hit the expert stuff on Pink Poodle. Stay left.

Narrow singletrack at Mount Kato.

2.6 Junction with High Line and Low Line. Stay on Low Line and descend on smooth dirt and steep switchback drops. Fun downhill to the bottom where the trail turns more grassy as it wanders through The Maze.

3.2 Split in the trail with the option to go back to the chalet, but you don't want to quit already, do you? Continue straight ahead and up the aptly named Staircase back to the top of the hill.

3.8 Hang a left and head back into the woods at the sign for Compressor. This is another fun descent with numerous sharp switchback turns and a fun last stretch on Cabin Run.

4.5 Back at trailhead. Now you're warmed up and ready for another lap. Grab a PowerBar at the rental shop and get back out there!

Eastwood Park

Location:	3.5 miles east of U.S. Highway 52 on U.S. Highway 14 in Rochester.
Distance:	4 miles on main loop; more available with alternate trails.
Time:	35–45 minutes.
Tread:	Hard-packed dirt singletrack.
Aerobic level:	Easy to moderate.
Technical difficulty:	Levels 2 to 3.
Hazards:	Trail stays muddy well after a rain; some loose rocks on a couple of descents; numerous log crossings.
Highlights:	Excellent tread condition; deep woods riding in the city; easy access; plenty of spur trails to explore.
Land status:	City of Rochester.
Maps:	USGS Rochester.
Access:	From Rochester at US 52, head east on US 14 for 3.5 miles. After passing County Road 22, the park will be on your right. The trail starts immediately adjacent to the picnic shelter at the west end of the parking lot.

Notes on the trail: The only negative to this trail is that it's not long enough. Easy access and superb trail conditions make Eastwood a good bet for a fun ride. The trail winds through dense woods on the fringes of a golf course and cornfields. Despite the traffic noise from the highway and the occasional glint of the sun from a pitching wedge, it feels like you're far away from the city. The trail isn't totally flat, but elevation gain is definitely minimal, with only a few rollers to keep things interesting. Tight turns with little room for error remind you to keep an eye on your bar ends or risk smashing a finger. I was initially concerned about not having a decent map of the park, but this ride hardly needs one. There is an easy-to-follow main trail and numerous offshoots that will keep you happy for a good two hours if you do a couple of extra laps. Throw in the uncrowded factor, and Eastwood serves up big mountain biking fun in a small package.

Eastwood Park

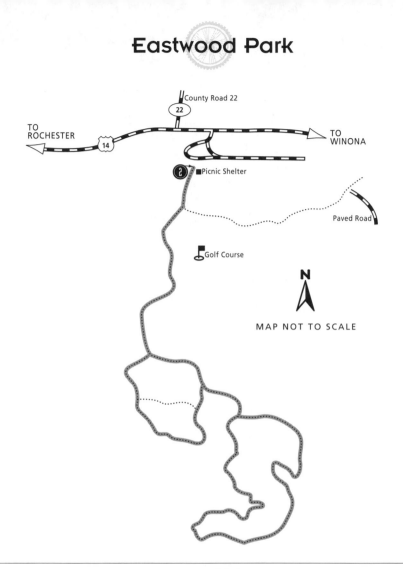

County Road 22

22

TO
ROCHESTER

14

TO
WINONA

Picnic Shelter

Paved Road

Golf Course

N

MAP NOT TO SCALE

The Ride

0.0   Trailhead. Ride to the start of the path just to the right (west) of the picnic shelter. Go past the first split to the left and continue up the gradual climb. The golf course is visible through the trees to the left. The biggest hill on the ride comes after the initial climb; there are some loose rocks to contend with and a mud pit at the bottom.

0.5   Break into a small clearing. The trail heads in the direction of the highway and then ducks back into the woods.

0.7   Go right at this fork in the trail. Trail loops around in a semi-circle. Turn right on the narrow path over a stick bridge, briefly through a portion of a field, then back to the woods. Stay left along the edge of the trees and along a steeper slope (watch this when it's wet).

1.0 Trail forks; go right, then right again at next fork.

1.1 Another fork; turn left and drop through a shallow valley across a creek bed and back up a moderate climb. Lots of logs to cross and narrow passages between trees. Trail exits into a small clearing and pushes through tall grasses back into the woods.

1.6 Arrive back where you began this little bonus loop. Turn right and go all the way down the hill and up the other side, back through the short cornfield path and back onto the main trail. Turn right and retrace the path to the beginning. Before reaching the trailhead, turn right at the spur trail you passed on the way in. Trail drops down a short, rocky descent and deposits you on a grass field behind the ballfield. Ride across and find the trail again in the woods on the other side. This is another short-lived path in the trees, visiting a peaceful stand of pines near the end, then back onto grass. Once again, ride across and into the woods, this time to a paved trail. I rode the pavement just to see where it was headed; after signs of a subdivision came into view, I turned around and headed back along the parking area roadway to the trailhead.

4.0 Back at trailhead.

Holzinger Lodge

Location:	Directly southwest of downtown Winona on the west side of U.S. Highway 61.
Distance:	10+ miles; distance will vary with different loops.
Time:	1.5–2 hours.
Tread:	Hard-packed dirt singletrack.
Aerobic level:	Moderate to strenuous.
Technical difficulty:	Levels 3 to 4.
Hazards:	Tight turns on skinny trail with steep drops to one side; a couple of tricky log crossings; some technical descents on the more difficult sections.
Highlights:	Excellent singletrack riding through deep woods; challenging terrain; splendid views from the top of the bluff; long or short loop options.
Land status:	City of Winona.
Maps:	USGS Winona West; park brochures.
Access:	From US 61, turn west on Huff Street and immediately north on West Lake Boulevard. Follow for 0.5 mile; Holzinger Lodge will be on the left up on a small hill. The trailhead is just to the north of the lodge. A sign is posted with park information and a trail map.

Notes on the trail: This was a *fun* ride: sweet singletrack riding on ideal trail conditions. The trail starts with a moderate climb to warm your legs, then rolls a bit before a cruise along some flatter sections to the base of Wildwood Climb. This is the start of an extended, sometimes-technical climb all the way to the top of the bluff. Along the way you'll be treated to tight turns, scary drops to the east, stream crossings, and just plain fun riding. There are a couple of breaks in the trees for a view of the valley, but prolonged gawking at the scenery has the potential to end in disaster. Use caution.

As the trail's elevation rises, you will ride through dense foliage crowding the path and through heavily wooded forest. Once at the top, fantastic views of Winona and the Mississippi River await. And the best part is, the

Holzinger Lodge

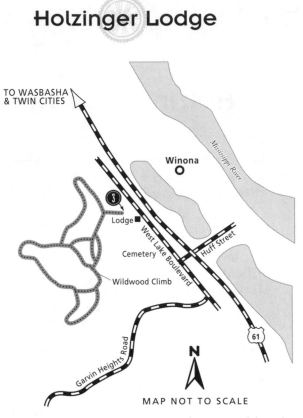

TO WASBASHA
& TWIN CITIES

Winona

Mississippi River

Lodge

West Lake Boulevard

Cemetery

Huff Street

Wildwood Climb

Garvin Heights Road

61

N

MAP NOT TO SCALE

ride isn't over. The trail continues to twist and turn and bend and snake along the blufftop until it finally deposits you into a residential neighborhood. Here you have the option of making a fast descent on paved roads to the bottom or going back down the way you came. If you are unfamiliar with this trail, it's very easy to get turned around or to miss the best turnoff on the way up. I had invaluable assistance from two young local riders, but if you don't have a leader, just explore! Holzinger is a great place to play. One more note: Detailed GPS mapping has been done of the trails. Check with Winona Area Mountain Bikers (507–452–4228) for the latest news.

The Ride

From the trailhead, ride north and loop around the first switchback, then head back in the direction you came from (south). As the trail passes the starting point, it begins a moderate, rocky climb. At about the 2-mile mark, the trail actually goes back downhill for a short distance, then turns off and rolls south. (This is a tricky part. I couldn't find this turn without help. Remember to keep riding south.) In the vicinity of the adjacent cemetery, the trail begins its long climb to the top near a huge cement cistern. A sign

The Brabbit brothers on the Holzinger Lodge Trail in Winona.

labeled WILDWOOD CLIMB assures you that you're on the right track. From here, it's just a hammerfest up, up, up to higher ground. I did the long loop; the mileage was around 10 miles. More or fewer miles can also be ridden depending on your mood and choice of routes.

Note: These trails are especially prone to erosion and wear. Trails that are already tired will suffer from irresponsible riding. If we don't treat the area right, the trails will be closed to use, and none of us want that. Always yield to hikers, wear your helmet, and don't go near the place when it's wet. Only ride on designated routes. Stay on the trail or stay home. Contact Winona Area Mountain Bikers for latest trail conditions: (507) 452–4228 (Adventure Cycle & Ski), or e-mail greg@wamb.com. Their word is gospel; if they say it's not a good day to ride, come back at a later date.

Richard J. Dorer Memorial Hardwood State Forest

The Dorer Forest stretches under several different management units from the far southeast corner of Minnesota to north of Red Wing. Most of these units are situated in the rolling bluffs and valleys along the Mississippi River. In fact, only three units of the forest are open to mountain biking, and all are very close to the river. This forest was established in 1961 as a tribute to Minnesota pioneers and veterans and to provide outdoor recreation, species diversity, and wildlife habitat. You're sure to enjoy the excellent riding on these trails that wind through hillsides cloaked in hickory, black walnut, oak, maple, and cherry. The challenging, rolling hills, combined with stunning views, make for a stellar riding experience.

Snake Creek Trail

Location:	9 miles south of Wabasha, directly west of U.S. Highway 61.
Distance:	10.4-mile loop.
Time:	1.5–2 hours.
Tread:	Hard-packed and gravel doubletrack.
Aerobic level:	Moderate +.
Technical difficulty:	Levels 2 to 3.
Hazards:	Loose rocks or sand; huge water bars on the first long downhill.
Highlights:	Variety of terrain; fine views of the valley; long downhills to reward your uphill efforts.
Land status:	State of Minnesota.
Maps:	USGS Wabasha South; state forest maps.
Access:	From US 61, turn west at the signs for Snake Creek Trail onto a gravel road. As the road curves to the right, *continue straight ahead* on the narrow field road to its end. Trail begins at the gate.

Notes on the trail: The Snake Creek Trail is wide doubletrack over its entire length and offers tread with loose rocks, sand, gravel, and hard-packed dirt. The rocks appear almost exclusively on the four big hills you'll be riding up or down. Technical difficulty is medium, but you will need to negotiate these sections well enough to avoid an unexpected endo (see Glossary). The field roads across the top of the ridge are packed and mostly smooth—a good place to really open 'er up. This is also where you'll find splendiferous views of the ridges and valleys of the surrounding area, especially scenic when draped in the colors of autumn. The first significant downhill is littered with balance-skewing rocks, and as a bonus has several large water bars built right into the trail. With the speed of the descent and the size of these things, you'll have the opportunity to get BIG air (even if you don't want to). The first one surprised me and nearly had me "riding" upside down! Use caution.

The first climb comes soon after the start and is more easily handled if you're properly warmed up. It is relatively long, with a steep enough grade to require some huffing. Ditto for the gravel road ascent from the bottom of the valley. Breathe deeply on the final descent to take in the

Snake Creek Trail

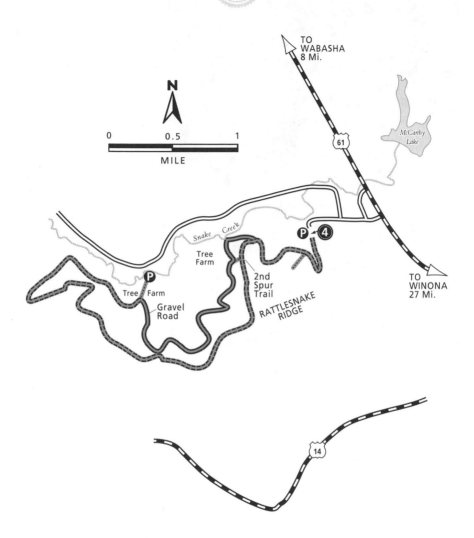

sweet scent wafting from dense pine stands. Wildlife, too, may present itself in the form of deer, wild turkey, hawks, or even the occasional owl.

The Ride

0.0   Ride past the gate onto a wide, grassy trail that turns quickly to gravel. Follow the switchback turn to the right, gradually climbing up from the valley. Keep an eye on the orange snowmobile trail markers. Continue past the first trail junction on your left and ride right through the clover field and back into the woods.

Snake Creek Trail in the Richard J. Dorer Memorial Hardwood State Forest.

.68   Continue past a second spur trail on your left. Remember that these trails are shared with ATVs and hikers.

1.3   Begin a medium-steep climb to the top of the ridge. Trail gets more technical the higher you go, then turns to hard-packed dirt on top.

1.9   Trail Ts at a crop field; go right for a few pedal strokes, then go left as the trail heads directly into open fields.

3.0   A Y in the trail; go left through a pine stand and more fields.

3.8   Ride back into the woods as the trail begins to point downhill. A couple of rollers await you for about 0.5 miles, and then get ready for a long descent littered with loose rocks. Use caution here as the combination of your high speed, gravel, and those huge water bars I mentioned earlier are the perfect ingredients for a nasty faceplant. Follow the trail to the right at the bottom of the hill and through the bottomlands of Snake Creek.

5.2   Junction with narrow gravel road and a tree farm off to the left. Take a right and begin climbing back up to the top of the bluff! This one is long and the gravel is deep—I was glad to get to the top. After catching your breath, turn left at the very same intersection you came in from after riding through the open fields.

Trail rolls up and down through mixed pine and hardwood forest.

8.0 Trail comes to a junction with another tree farm; go right.

8.3 A fork appears in the road; take a left and drop quickly back to lower elevations. Again, watch the loose rocks and keep your speed within your ability to control the bike. Follow the trail to the next junction (your first climb up the ridge) and go left, retracing your tracks back to the trailhead. **Note:** The second spur trail you passed on the way in at 0.68 is available as an alternate—and more enjoyable—return route if you'd like a change of scenery.

10.4 Back at trailhead.

Plowline Trail
(Cherry Hill)

Location:	Directly northwest of Winona adjacent to County Road 23.
Distance:	7.6-mile loop.
Time:	1.5 hours.
Tread:	Gravel and dirt double- and singletrack.
Aerobic level:	Moderate +, with one strenuous section.
Technical difficulty:	Levels 2 to 4.
Hazards:	Loose rocks; steep descents with narrow lines and assorted debris.
Highlights:	Excellent loop on good tread; challenging terrain; fun, well-maintained trails; great views of the valleys.
Land status:	State of Minnesota.
Maps:	USGS Winona West; state forest maps.
Access:	From Winona, go north on U.S. Highway 61 to U.S. Highway 14. Take US 14 west 5.5 miles to the little town of Stockton. Turn north on CR 23 for just over 2 miles to Hillsdale Township Road 6. Go right across the tracks and follow the narrow dirt road for the high side of 1 mile to the parking area. There are two gates here; take the one that leads uphill.

Notes on the trail: The Plowline Trail (Cherry Hill to locals), similar to the Trout Valley trails to the north, is another great place to play on the scenic bluffs along the river. Trail conditions are excellent and there are three overlooks along the route for you to check out the incredible views of the surrounding valleys. It's especially cool to be here when the bald eagles flock to the area in huge numbers. After the initial climb from the trailhead, the path is generally flat to rolling as it winds through 7 miles of doubletrack along the wooded blufftop. These trails are also home to the annual Cherry Bomb mountain bike race, sponsored by the experts at Adventure Cycle and Ski in Winona. An additional 2.5 miles of singletrack have been built to the south of the main trail, so be sure to check that out while you're there. More information can be found on the Web site for the Winona Area Mountain Bikes, www.wamb.com.

Plowline Trail

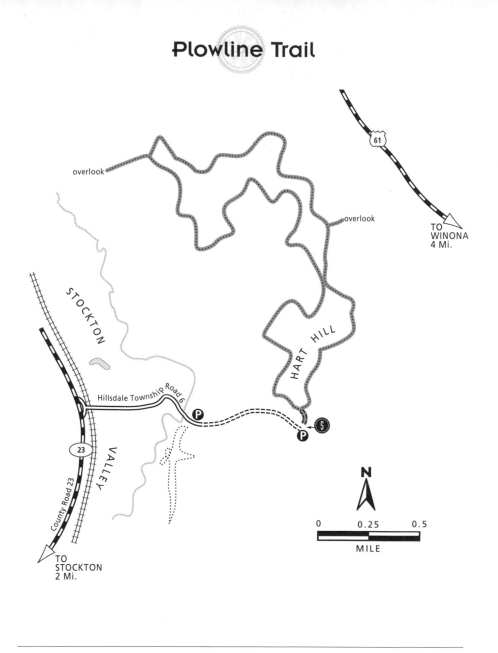

The Ride

0.0   Warm up first, then ride around the gate and head immediately uphill. Hang a left at the first junction at the top of the hill. The trail begins its winding journey along the top of Stockton Valley. Follow the path all the way to the junction with the first overlook at mile four.

4.0   Go left for some fine views of the valley and neighboring hills. After that, cross a hiking trail and wind your way to . . .

5.0   The next overlook. This time you get a first-rate view of the Mississippi River Valley in all its glory. The river fans out in several backwater sections, and it's fun to see the many different mini-ecosystems that the river supports. This is a great place to spot eagles.

5.7   Continue down the trail, then lean left where the trails merge and curve back toward the starting point. Stay left at the first four-way junction, then go right at the next one and down the hill to the trailhead.

7.6   Back at trailhead.

Trout Valley Trail

Location:	Nearly dead center between Wabasha and Winona, 2 miles west of U.S. Highway 61.
Distance:	7.6-mile loop.
Time:	1–1.5 hours.
Tread:	A mix of loose rocks, gravel, and hard-packed dirt single- and doubletrack.
Aerobic level:	Moderate to strenuous, with some easy sections on top.
Technical difficulty:	Levels 2 to 4 +.
Hazards:	Continuous loose rocks, water bars, gullies, and other detritus on the hills; great views can distract your concentration; look and listen for ATVs, hikers, and horses; prepare for long, technical climbs and descents.
Highlights:	Fantabulous views of both sides of the bluff; fun riding through the trees and fields on top; challenging to satisfy your training demands; quiet and uncrowded.
Land status:	State of Minnesota; private.
Maps:	USGS Weaver; state forest maps.
Access:	Signs are posted on US 61 for Trout Valley Trail; turn onto County Road 29 and follow the gravel road 1.5 miles to the trailhead parking area. (The entrance road will turn into Winona County Road 31—stay on course until you reach the trailhead.)

Notes on the trail: This is another well-used trail, so there is no danger of taking a wrong turn or getting lost. Some portions are actually too well-used by ATVs, as the gravel has a tendency to become rather deep and it feels like you're pedaling through sand. As if that wasn't hard enough, the trail instantly climbs a good half-mile at a steep grade with loose rocks. Warm up properly down below before heading out on this one. The trail is shared with hikers, horses, and ATVs, so yield when you should and ride smart.

There are two climbs on this ride that will test your strength and your sanity. Grades are steep and littered with loose rocks nearly the whole

Trout Valley Trail

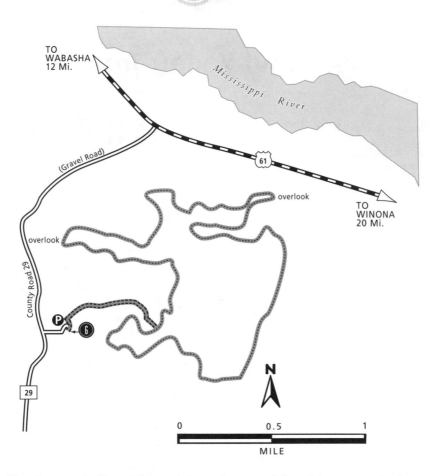

TO
WABASHA
12 Mi.

Mississippi River

(Gravel Road)

61

overlook

TO
WINONA
20 Mi.

overlook

County Road 29

P

6

29

N

| 0 | 0.5 | 1 |

MILE

way. The descent halfway through begs for speed, but it's extremely dangerous to get going too fast. These hills used every bit of my skills just to survive, but you might have an easier time. If you can ride the entire way up either of the climbs, you're superhuman and should be wearing a cape.

The flats on top of the bluff are a blast, gently rolling through aspen, oak, and pine and then around a tree farm. Plan on stopping at the overlooks for the views. I've run out of superlatives to describe the sight! Looking over the Mississippi is especially interesting with all the different personalities the river reveals.

The Ride

0.0   Ride past the gate and up a wide gravel trail. Be ready for said gravel to be deep and loose, making for difficult riding as the

The Mississippi River Valley near Winona.

grade begins its rise. Trail is shared with hikers, ATVs, and horses, so use caution. Continue past the first spur at 0.3 mile and keep climbing.

0.65 Top of the hill. Take in some oxygen and turn left, following the trail alongside a tree farm. Trail becomes hard-packed dirt and grass. Look for the ever-present eagles and hawks soaring above. An immature bald eagle touched down on a wooden fence post 100 yards in front of me here. Very cool.

1.4 Check out the first scenic overlook of Trout Creek Valley and all that elevation you just gained. Trail enters a fun section heavy with oak of different flavors, aspen, and pine. This ride's scenery is extra beautiful in the fall; ride it then or come back and ride it again.

3.6 Stop here and consider what you'll miss if you don't take a left. Go that way and bask in spectacular views of both sides of this bluff. On the river side, get as close as you dare to the edge and discover just how high you've ridden your bike. Take some time to enjoy the vista of Wisconsin's bluffs and study the meanderings of the Mississippi. Then go to the other side and relax on the handy bench overlooking heavily wooded valleys and crop fields.

Come back to your senses and follow the trail as it points down hill. Prepare yourself for a nearly 1-mile descent over rocky, steep tread. Water bars and lots of loose rocks await. Pick a line and stick with it; control your speed or expect to face plant. This downhill is almost as tiring as going up the other way. At the bottom, go right down a narrow gravel road and ride past another gate and an alternate parking area. Then the trail goes back up again! Another long one, almost a mile, and just as rocky as the initial climb.

5.8 Follow the trail along the tree farm again all the way to . . .

7.0 The top of the first hill. Go left and head downhill, using the same common sense that got you safely down that other slope.

7.6 Back at trailhead.

Mendota Trail

Location:	Along south side of Minnesota River adjacent to MN Highway 13 between MN Highway 55 and I–494.
Distance:	8.7 miles out and back.
Time:	25–45 minutes.
Tread:	0.4 miles on pavement; remaining 8.3 miles on wide gravel trail.
Aerobic level:	Easy.
Technical difficulty:	Level 1.
Hazards:	Some loose gravel to watch for in places.
Highlights:	Great beginner ride or easy spin on flat terrain. Fun, quiet ride along the river flats.
Land status:	Fort Snelling State Park.
Maps:	USGS St. Paul SW; state park brochures.
Access:	Begin at parking area on MN 13 just west of Sibley Historic Site and town of Mendota, near MN 110 and MN 55.

A winding river trail in Mendota.

Mendota Trail

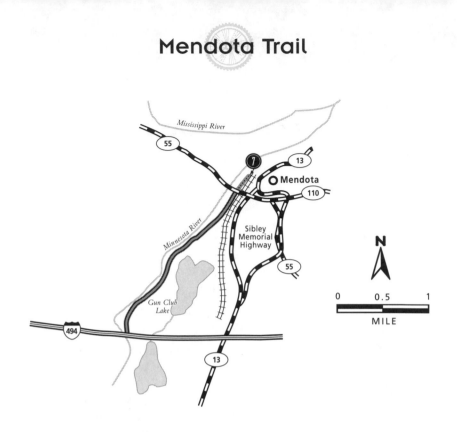

Notes on the trail: This is the first of several Minnesota River Valley rides in this book. It's a relaxing ride, starting out at the Sibley House and heading right down to the river. Some cool singletrack trails branch off along the riverbank toward St. Paul, while the main gravel path hugs a rail bed in the opposite direction. The trail takes you through dense woodland that is jungle-like in the summer. There is always a healthy crop of nettles down in the valley, so be aware of that. Just a slight brush with one of those leaves and that burning sensation stays with you the rest of the day. Tread condition is excellent and the trail is flat as a pancake. There is also direct access to the next ride if you want to double the mileage.

The Ride

0.0 Ride east toward Mendota on sidewalk next to Minnesota's oldest European-American settlement with 1800's-era limestone houses. Go left on Water Street and curve down past the Sibley House. Turn right under the railroad trestle and into Fort Snelling State Park. The Minnesota River is right in front of you. Take the trail to the left, riding underneath MN 55.

1.2 Trail bends away from the bluff and into heavily wooded river flats. Huge cottonwoods, elms, maple, and ash trees live here. Trail is a flat, relatively wide gravel road.

2.2 Cross cement bridge over drainage from the river's flood plain. (Watch for herons.) The structure above and to your right is the airport's strobe beacon for inbound planes.

3.1 Pass under I–494 bridge. (It is possible to ride past the cement bridge columns and clamber up the opposite bank to a paved bike trail that leads to Bloomington or Eagan.) The ride reverses at this point and returns on the trail to Mendota. Easy access at this point to Ride 8.

8.7 Back at trailhead.

Fort Snelling State Park

Location:	Along south bank of Minnesota River between I–494 and Cedar Avenue.
Distance:	6 miles out and back.
Time:	15–30 minutes.
Tread:	A mix of wide gravel and dirt singletrack and mud.
Aerobic level:	Easy +.
Technical difficulty:	Levels 1 to 2.
Hazards:	Some roots and rocks to negotiate; gooey mud after a rain.
Highlights:	A fun and scenic ride along the river through thick woods and marshland.
Land status:	Fort Snelling State Park.
Maps:	USGS St. Paul SW; state park brochures.
Access:	This ride is best started from the Cedar Avenue bike ramp and boat landing. From the south, take Silver Bell Road north from MN Highway 13 to Nicols Road. Follow this road to the parking area underneath the Cedar Avenue bridge. The trail begins at the base of the bike ramp heading east.

Notes on the trail: Just a fun, flat trip through the river valley. The path starts out as a wide doubletrack, then narrows to sweet dirt singletrack in the woods. The trail hugs the riverbank closely as it twists around giant cottonwood trees. Try to stay away from this trail in the spring or after a good rain; the mud will claim both you and your bike. This route offers easy access to Ride 7. Many people combine these two routes into one longer ride; they are separated in this book to highlight each ride's features.

The Ride

0.0   Begin riding east at the base of the bike ramp, following a dirt trail through the trees. A sign with a map of the park is posted on your left as you continue on to a wider, gravel trail.

Fort Snelling State Park

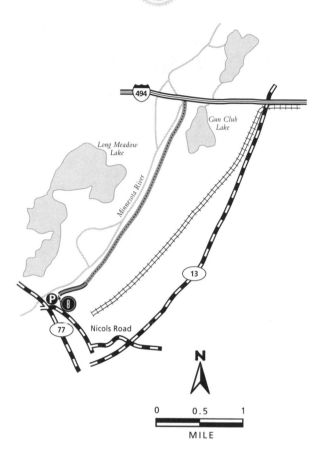

0.4 Cross wooden bridge and a small creek. Trail narrows and turns to hard-packed dirt singletrack on the other side of bridge. Ride into area heavily wooded with silver maple, ash, and elm. This section gets very soft and sticky when wet. Best to avoid this trail altogether after a rain to limit damage to trail.

0.59 Cross a second wooden bridge. Look and listen for different types of critters, such as deer, bald eagles, and herons.

1.6 Cross another wooden bridge. If you've ridden this far after a heavy rain, you are probably struggling through an oozing, pulsating, bike-eating pit of no return. It's best to stay away from here when it's wet. Do not dare to test the Swamp Thing.

2.8 Trail turns back into a wide gravel path, straight and flat to I-494.

3.0 Junction with the bottom of I-494. Do a U-turn and retrace your tracks, or keep going to Ride 7 and Mendota.

6.0 Back at trailhead.

River Valley Rover

Location:	Along the Minnesota River bluff and wetland area between Cedar Avenue and I–35W.
Distance:	9.3-mile loop.
Time:	1.25–1.5 hours.
Tread:	6.1 miles dirt singletrack; 3.2 miles paved road.
Aerobic level:	A little of each, easy to strenuous.
Technical difficulty:	Levels 1 to 4.
Hazards:	Deep, loose sand; sticky mud if wet; several stream crossings; carniverous mosquitoes.
Highlights:	Fun ride along riverbank, then sweet, rolling singletrack through the bluff woods. Challenging climbs and a couple of screamin' downhills on well-maintained trail.
Land status:	U.S. Fish & Wildlife Service; City of Blooming-ton; private.
Maps:	USGS Bloomington.
Access:	Begin this loop at the parking area at bottom of the Old Cedar Avenue hill on the north side of the river. Ride across bridge to reach start of ride.

Notes on the trail: This ride is a highlight of the river valley trails. You get a great chance to warm up on the old Cedar Avenue bridge and its adjoining paved road, then jump onto dirt singletrack right on the edge of the river. The trail stays close to the water all the way to a drainage inlet, then tracks off into the woods. It gets better when you meet with the popular bluff trail at Bloomington's southern border. A mix of hard-packed dirt and stretches of deep sand lets you use some different skills, and there are several steep climbs and descents to give your adrenaline a little spike. One downside to this trail is the crowds, especially on weekends. It's easy to run into or get plowed over by another rider. This is also a trail that may be closed someday due to some people's lack of respect for other users and from plans to make this into another "multiple use" trail for the masses. More on that in Ride 11.

River Valley Rover

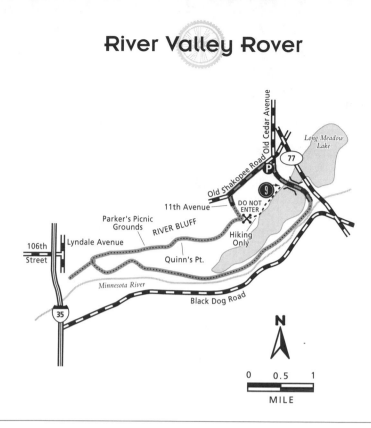

The Ride

0.0 Ride on old bridge across the channel between the larger sections of Long Meadow Lake. Imagine quieter days when this was the bridge carrying auto traffic to the southern communities as you look to your left at the present-day exodus.

0.68 The road ends abruptly at the edge of the river. To your left is a bike ramp leading to the other side, to your right is a wide gravel trail. Go right. The trail follows along the riverbank and narrows to hard-packed dirt singletrack.

1.9 Pass the Black Dog power plant on south side of river. Ride through a stand of baby aspen and willow brush. Watch for loose sand in spots.

2.0 Lots of loose, deep sand to negotiate and some whoop-de-dos.

3.3 Bear right to avoid riding into a channel of the river. Ride along until you find a place to cross the channel (several options exist depending on trail conditions and your confidence level). Your goal is to get back to the main trail at the riverbank.

4.5 Stream crossing, then navigate through deadfall until trail reappears away from river.

4.6 Junction with main bluff trail. Lyndale Avenue (and access to Ride 11) is 0.42 mile down the left fork; Bloomington city streets are up the trail straight ahead, and you're going to the right. Climb on hard-packed dirt and point yourself east back toward Cedar Avenue.

5.2 Steep climb with deep sand. Use your strongest legs to get to the top.

5.4 Stream crossing.

5.5 Take the low road.

6.0 You made it to higher ground (and great views of the valley) at Parker's Picnic Grounds. Follow the trail back down a steep hill; use caution.

6.4 Steep climb to Quinn's Point; follow the trail to . . .

6.6 Take the right fork back down the hill. Turn and ride uphill again past the Minnesota Valley National Wildlife Refuge sign. Do not ride into the refuge at this point. Bikes are not allowed between here and Cedar Avenue. It is a federal violation to ride on this refuge, which could result in a $700 fine and possible impounding of your bike. Rangers are enforcing this regularly. **Stay on the trail or stay home.** Don't be tempted by the tracks of ruffians who have ignored the rules. Keep climbing up to Indian Mounds Park (11th Avenue). Follow 11th Avenue north, working your way to Old Shakopee Road. Take it east to . . .

8.8 Old Cedar Avenue. Go right and down the hill to the parking area.

9.3 Back at Trailhead.

Note: The section of this ride along the Minnesota River is slated to be the future alignment for the Minnesota Valley State Trail. Currently, the trail is only partially maintained and designated as an informal multiple-use path (hikers and bikers). Someday, it'll probably be paved, or at least turned into a wide, flat gravel trail. Enjoy it now before the masses descend, and *yield* to other users.

Bass Ponds Loop

Location: On the north side of the Minnesota River immediately east of Cedar Avenue.
Distance: 3 miles.
Time: 15–25 minutes.
Tread: Entire loop is on medium to wide gravel trail.
Aerobic level: Easy.
Technical difficulty: Level 1.
Hazards: Occasional loose gravel; slippery goose droppings.
Highlights: Relaxed ride through wildlife-abundant area near river; great beginner loop.
Land status: U.S. Fish and Wildlife Service.
Maps: USGS Bloomington; refuge brochures.
Access: Start this ride at the north end of the Old Cedar Avenue Bridge, about 0.5 mile south of Old Shakopee Road in Bloomington. Easy access from MN Highway 77 just to the east.

Notes on the trail: If you're a beginner, come to Bass Ponds. If you're a racer, it's still a great place for a spin. The whole trail is on wide, smooth gravel with no hills. The section west of Cedar Avenue is a great place to spot different bird species, and the east side takes you around the ponds and close to Long Meadow Lake. There are always ducks and herons and muskrats hanging around here in summer. There may be a good supply of hikers on weekends, so don't use this area to redline your speedometer.

The Ride

0.0 Trailhead. Ride across the road, past the gate, and onto a wide gravel trail heading east toward the highway. *This is a very popular trail for hikers and birdwatchers. Respect their space. Control your speed.*

0.54 Ride under MN 77 through a tricky section of dirt trail. Use caution. Immediately after the bridge you will need to hike your bike up a short stairway leading up from the river. Continue east on the path, riding along the Hog Back Ridge Pond. These ponds were

Bass Ponds Loop

created by the Izaak Walton League for rearing bass in 1926. The ponds remained in operation for over thirty years, and were eventually sold to the U.S. Fish and Wildlife Service.

1.3   Junction with trail to Big Bass Pond; turn right. Ride across a finely crafted wooden bridge and lean to the left. *Do not ride onto the interpretive hiking trail to your right. This area is closed to bicycles.*

1.5   Ride past the parking area and information kiosks (after stopping to read a little background information on the ponds) and back toward the trailhead. Choose a different pond and explore this small but unique area.

3.0   Back at trailhead.

Bloomington Ferry Trail

Update: This trail is one of the most popular trails in the metro area and is heavily traveled by lots of fat tires. It is also in danger of being closed to mountain bikes. The trail passes through at least two private land areas, and the rest is largely the domain of the United States Fish and Wildlife Service. The Minnesota Department of Natural Resources has its sights on this corridor to continue construction of the Minnesota Valley State Trail, connecting to additional segments upstream. At this point, no one is sure if the trail will be surfaced with crushed limestone or pavement. If paved, look for this special area to be inundated with hordes of in-line skaters and strollers and the usual array of weekend passersby. Ugh. This is a really bad idea. We've got hundreds of miles of paved bike paths all over the Twin Cities, and damn few unique natural areas like this one. When did it become so difficult to just leave things alone?

Much of the angst toward those of the knobby-tired nature originates from unpleasant encounters out on the trail. Hikers wandered these woods long before bikes, and the area is still loaded with wildlife and is sensitive to intrusion. (I'm not sure how dozing through here with paving machinery is going to help matters, but so goes the vision of the governing agencies.) The banzai riding style of more than a few has instilled the following thought into the minds of the FWS and hiking groups: Mountain bikes are dangerous, harm the environment, and should not be allowed. Well, they are dangerous when riders come screaming around blind corners at warp speed and plow over a scout troop. If you want to race, do it at a race on a closed course. Other users enjoy the river flats, too, and shouldn't be afraid to head down there for fear of personal injury. Our own behavior may shut down our favorite trail. However, there is a possibility that a separate singletrack trail will be built adjacent to the State Trail to accommodate mountain bikes. Your opinions matter tremendously. The FWS, the City of Bloomington, and the DNR are all places to contact to make yourself heard. Also, the no-brainer deeds like not littering and volunteering to maintain the trail go a long way. The Minnesota Off-Road Cyclists Club has made great strides in protecting this trail. Check them out at www.morcmtb.com.

Location:	Along the north banks of Minnesota River between I–35 and the old Bloomington Ferry Bridge (County Road 18).
Distance:	13.7 miles.
Time:	1.5–1.75 hours.

Tread:	12.8 miles dirt singletrack; 0.9 mile wide gravel trail.
Aerobic level:	Moderate +.
Technical difficulty:	Levels 2 to 3 +.
Hazards:	Loose sand; inlets from river to cross; technical log crossings; hike-a-bike sections to and from the raft. Area is prone to flooding; avoid riding after heavy rain.
Highlights:	Long, challenging singletrack ride next to the river. Well-maintained trail that tests your handling skills and offers some of the best scenery in the valley.
Land status:	City of Bloomington; U.S. Fish and Wildlife Service; private.
Maps:	USGS Bloomington.
Access:	This out-and-back route begins at the parking area on the north side of the old Bloomington Ferry Bridge. Access from Bloomington Ferry and Auto Club Roads, or ride across from the south on a newer bike/hike path. Trail heads off from the left corner of the parking lot as you ride toward the bridge.

Notes on the trail: Even though this ride lacks any change in elevation, it is still one of the favorites in all the land. Exquisite hard-packed single-track follows the banks of the Minnesota River in a winding, twisty manner through lush vegetation and dense woodland. An abundance of stream crossings over homemade stick bridges challenge your skills, and the raft portage over Nine Mile Creek is a one-of-a-kind experience. This section alone is a satisfying out-and-back ride, and direct access to Ride 9 allows for lengthy mileage and a solid day of dirt-filled fun.

The Ride

0.0 Ride toward bridge and off the pavement onto the dirt trail. Use caution on this relatively steep descent and watch for bike-swallowing erosion gullies. Enter immediately into heavily wooded flood plain area. *This trail is shared with hikers. Ride smart.*

1.7 Stream crossing through a ravine. Be alert for roots in the trail, along with downed logs and trees.

2.3 Cross a stream over a handmade cairn of logs and sticks. Use caution.

2.6 Ride past grain elevators and barge operations across the river. Trail along here hugs the edge of the bank; don't lean too far to the right.

3.2 Pass under the old swinging bridge river crossing for auto traffic and trains.

Bloomington Ferry Trail

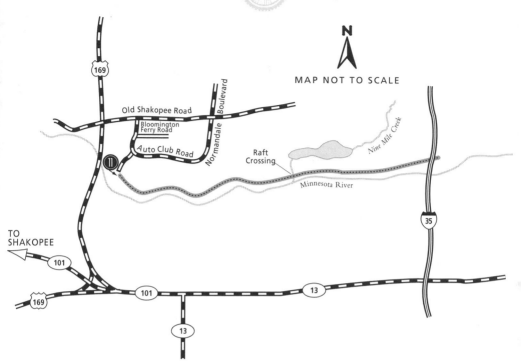

3.3 Go over another log/stick stream crossing, and then another after that.

3.5 Yet another log bridge over a stream. How are your technical skills holding up?

5.0 The loose sand starts in this area. Power through it! It stretches 50 to 75 yards.

5.2 Wide stream crossing.This is where Nine Mile Creek reaches its ninth mile and empties into the Minnesota River. A handy raft made of plastic 30-gallon drums and pallets is available (at time of this writing) for you to get over to the other side. Scramble carefully down and onto the raft and pull yourself along with the center cable strung between the trees, humming the "Dueling Banjoes" tune from *Deliverance* as you go. Use great caution getting on and off the raft. If you do start to sink into the goo, at least make sure your bike makes it out okay.

6.1 Trail evolves into a wide, hard-packed gravel path, then a wider service road. Follow this all the way to the I–35W bridge.

6.9 Arrive at the freeway bridge. There is access to Ride 9 right over there on the far side of the Lyndale Avenue parking area. This route turns around here and heads back west.

13.7 Back at trailhead.

New Bridge Trail

Location:	On the north side of the Minnesota River riding west from County Road 18 (old Ferry Bridge). *This trail passes underneath the "new" Bloomington Ferry Bridge, hence the trail's unimaginative name. The new bridge is already several years old, but we locals are in the habit of calling it new to distinguish it from the old one.*
Distance:	2.2-mile out and back trail.
Time:	10–15 minutes.
Tread:	Mix of gravel and dirt singletrack.
Aerobic level:	Easy.
Technical difficulty:	Levels 1 to 2.
Hazards:	May be some loose sand or a deer crossing your path.
Highlights:	Easy access trail through wooded river flats; great views of the underbelly of a freeway bridge.
Land status:	Cities of Bloomington and Eden Prairie; U.S. Fish and Wildlife Service.
Maps:	USGS Bloomington, Eden Prairie.
Access:	Park in same lot as Ride 11 and ride west on wide gravel trail.

Notes on the trail: I thought this was kind of a fun ride for folks who have traveled this part of the valley for many years. The trailhead sits at a location that was a major river crossing point for a bazillion cars heading to and from work each day. The river would rise and flood the road almost every spring, forcing the hordes to find another way across, and the valley would plunge into silence. With all the cars on the big bridge now, the road has been transformed into a bike/pedestrian path. The short trail for this ride used to be a footpath for fishing (and partying) crowds to access the river, then it was made wider and reverberated with heavy equipment during bridge construction. Now it's a nice little trail that takes you underneath the new bridge and wanders through some funky wooded areas on the other side. I sometimes use it as a warm-up ride before taking off on the Ferry Trail.

New Bridge Trail

N

0 1 2
MILES

169

Riverview Road

Old Shakopee Road

Minnesota River

12

P

Bloomington
Ferry Road

101

The Ride

0.0 Begin riding westbound from parking lot on wide gravel trail. This was a heavily used access road during construction of the new river bridge.

0.7 Arrive directly underneath the recently completed Ferry Bridge. Admire the handiwork of yet another epic construction project, then continue on the trail along the riverbank. Trail turns to hard-packed dirt as it enters forested river flats. *If you decide to take a right turn under the bridge, you will follow the northbound traffic flow and ride into a small pond/floodplain.*

1.1 Trail enters large, open field. *This is private property. Turn around and go back.*

2.2 Back at trailhead.

Note: This is another trail where mountain bikes aren't welcome uses. If you ride it, go slow and *do not* enter the private land on the west end.

St. Lawrence Unit
(Wet Side)

Location:	Approximately 4 miles southwest of Jordan on the north side of U.S. Highway 169.
Distance:	4.4-mile loop.
Time:	18–30 minutes.
Tread:	0.5 mile gravel road; 3.9 miles grass and dirt trail.
Aerobic level:	Moderate.
Technical difficulty:	Levels 1 to 3.
Hazards:	Really bumpy sections early and late in ride; possible flooding when wet.
Highlights:	Extremely quiet; scenic ride through river flats and historic town site.
Land status:	State of Minnesota.
Maps:	USGS Jordan West; map at park office.
Access:	Drive 4 miles south of Jordan on US 169 to Park Boulevard. Turn right, cross the railroad tracks, and proceed to the park headquarters. Pay daily fee ($4) and, if office is staffed, inquire about parking. I started this ride at the park office, but alternate starting points are available on the way in.

Notes on the trail: This is an interesting chunk of the extensive Minnesota River Valley State Recreation Area and a fun one for riding. There is more open prairie-type land here, and the trails bring you through high grasses on the way to the wooded banks of the river. The State Corridor Trail was in mediocre condition for bikes, and you'll encounter bone-jarring horse tracks for a good distance. There's wildlife all over the place, more than usual because of a mix of habitats. Look for deer, grouse, squirrels, herons, ducks, hawks, and a bevy of other birds. I separated this ride and the next one mainly for the settings, but they can easily be combined for a continuous loop.

St. Lawrence Unit (Wet Side)

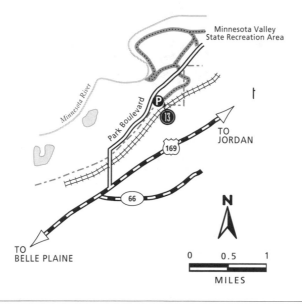

The Ride

0.0   Ride north (right) from the park office on the gravel road until you arrive at . . .

0.24 A wide, grassy trail that leads from both sides of the road; turn left. Hikers and horses also use this trail; be sure to yield to them. Go straight (lean left) at the first fork you come to. Trail starts out very bumpy and then blends with forested dirt path with the river over to your right.

0.70 Fork in the road. A left will dump you onto the gravel road you came in on, so take a right here. A map is posted on a sign for assistance. Trail descends a bit and snakes through two small ponds. Stop here and commune with nature. Only the faint drone of traffic ruins an otherwise idyllic setting.

1.3   Pass campground on your left.

1.6   This is the Trail Center. Picnic tables and an open area can be found here, as well as maps and information. Continuing straight ahead will take you to Belle Plaine; this ride turns right and loops back toward the river. At the T intersection, take a right. Rough trail here with lots o' horse tracks and deep sand. Be ready.

3.7   Go straight at this fork, passing by the historic town of St. Lawrence. Turn right when trail meets gravel road and continue back to the park office.

4.4   Back at park office and trailhead.

St. Lawrence Unit
(Dry Side)

Location:	Same as Ride 13.
Distance:	1.3-mile loop.
Time:	10–20 minutes.
Tread:	0.4 mile gravel road; 0.9 mile rolling, grassy trail.
Aerobic level:	Easy.
Technical difficulty:	Levels 1 to 2.
Hazards:	A possible deep bump or two; otherwise this is a pretty tame trail.
Highlights:	Fun ride through unique river valley ecosystem with aged oaks and thick sumac groves.
Land status:	State of Minnesota.
Maps:	USGS Jordan West; park maps.
Access:	See Ride 13.

Notes on the trail: This section of the two St. Lawrence rides is short, but I liked the remote feeling of the trail. Big oak trees are scattered along the trail, and there is a large, dense stand of sumac that's fun to ride through, especially in the fall. You can connect to more trail riding at the gravel road, or ride the road itself for long, flat miles.

The Ride

0.0 Begin ride as you did on Ride 13 at the park office. Go right on the gravel road to . . .

0.24 Take a right onto a wide, grassy trail directly across from the turn you made on the previous trail. Trail is in better overall condition for bikes on this side, and there are not as many mosquitoes! These are great cross-country ski trails; be sure to come back and try them out.

1.1 Go right at the fork and reach the gravel road. Turn right again and head back to the start.

1.3 Back at trailhead. Short and sweet.

St. Lawrence Unit (Dry Side)

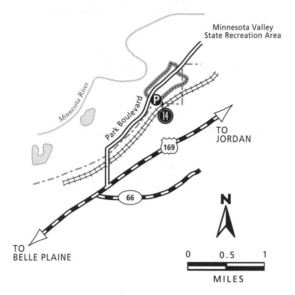

Minnesota Valley
State Recreation Area

Minnesota River

Park Boulevard

P

14

169

TO
JORDAN

66

N

TO
BELLE PLAINE

0   0.5   1

MILES

Louisville Swamp

Location:	Between Shakopee and Jordan on the river side of U.S. Highway 169.
Distance:	10.2-mile loop.
Time:	1–1.25 hours.
Tread:	Hard-packed gravel, grass, and dirt double-track.
Aerobic level:	Moderate.
Technical difficulty:	Levels 2 to 3.
Hazards:	Loose gravel and rocks; mud and water on trail; possible flooding; big swamp means lots o' big mosquitoes (bring Bug-B-Gone).
Highlights:	One of the most historic areas in the river valley; uncrowded; flat ride along river.
Land status:	U.S. Fish and Wildlife Service.
Maps:	USGS Jordan East; trail brochure at trailhead or refuge office.
Access:	Trailhead is approximately 3.5 miles south of Shakopee on US 169. Turn right (west) from US 169 at 145th Street (sign for Louisville Swamp). Proceed across railroad tracks and into parking lot on the left. The huge field with the funky buildings in the distance is the Renaissance Festival site, a grand time when you're not pushing the pedals. The Little Prairie and Mazomani Trails are for hiking only.

Notes on the trail: Louisville is a nice trail that brings you close to a rare woodland area, a historic homestead, and right along the banks of the Minnesota River. The first half of the ride is on wide gravel trail that is usually in good condition. The hiking trails look inviting, but that's what they're for, so stay your course. God help you if you linger too long in this section; the mosquitoes are not of this Earth. Only your bike will remain. After looping around to the river, the trail becomes a bit more primitive but still very rideable. You're bound to encounter horse tracks here that will rattle your bones. The State Corridor Trail offers even more mileage if you so desire.

Louisville Swamp

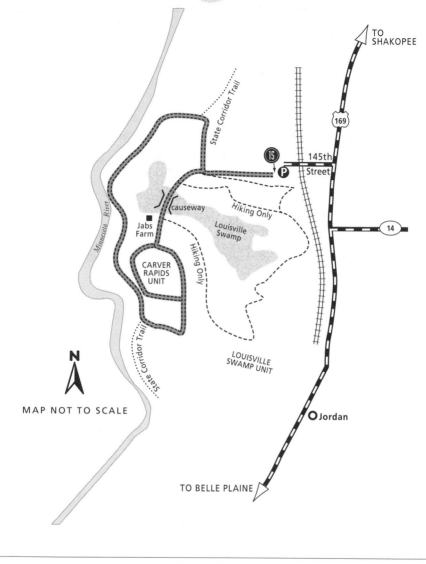

The Ride

0.0 Ride to south end of parking lot to information kiosk. Read interesting historical notes on the area and proceed on the hard-packed gravel trail (State Corridor Trail). Ride past the junction where the state trail turns north, continue straight ahead. You will pass the Little Prairie Trail and then the Mazomani Trail.

2.0	Cross a man-made causeway over the Louisville Swamp. If it's spring, this is probably flooded.
2.5	Pass historic Jabs Farm and outlet for Mazomani Trail.
3.2	Turn left here and ride the eastern leg of the Carver Rapids Unit. You can go right here, also, and the trail will deposit you in the same place.
4.3	Trail turns to the right and connects to the State Corridor Trail on the left (south).
5.3	Turn right on the state trail, passing a secluded campsite along the river.
7.8	Trail turns east and meets another junction; go right and follow main trail back to parking area.
10.2	Back at trailhead.

Lake Elmo Park Reserve

Location:	1 mile north of I–94 on County Road 19 (Keats Avenue).
Distance:	Choose any distance to your liking: 8 miles of trail to explore.
Time:	10 minutes to an hour or more.
Tread:	A mix of hard-packed singletrack and wide, grassy trail.
Aerobic level:	Easy +.
Technical difficulty:	Level 2.
Hazards:	May be some loose sand or gravel; a tendency to ride off the trail while looking at the abundant wildlife.
Highlights:	Abundant wildlife; rolling terrain through forest and prairie; uncrowded trails.
Land status:	Washington County Parks.
Maps:	USGS Lake Elmo; best map is in the park brochure available at the entrance station.
Access:	Enter the park 1 mile north of I–94 on Keats Avenue. After parting with $4 for a daily pass at the entrance station (season passes also available), proceed approximately 0.25 mile north to a parking area on the left side of the road.

Notes on the trail: This is an enjoyable short ride in one of our nicer regional parks. There are nice views of Eagle Point Lake from the woods, and trails are generally in good condition. One drawback is the presence of horses, because of what they leave behind. Even worse than the piles of crap are the horse tracks. The incessant bumps ruin a good ride. This is a beautiful setting, however, and a great place to spend a day. There are also plenty of paved miles for a relaxing cruise.

The Ride

0.0 Trailhead. *Trail is shared with hikers and horses. Use caution.* There are a variety of options available right from the get-go. On this

Lake Elmo Park Reserve

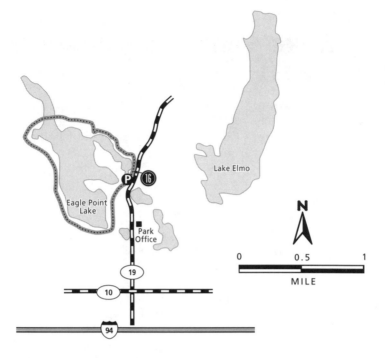

particular day I did a quick 4-mile loop around Eagle Point Lake and passed several other trails along the way. This area is perfect for exploring. Since there isn't a designated trail to follow, just ride! Go left or go right at the trailhead, then choose one of a dozen different spin-off trails.

Eighty percent of the 3.5 square miles that encompass Lake Elmo Park Reserve are set aside for preservation and/or protection. This is evident as you ride through the prairie and forest that will eventually look as they did prior to the mid-1800s when the first settlers arrived. Camping, fishing, hiking, horseback riding, and other activities are also available as diversions to your riding.

Afton Alps Ski Area

Location:	21 miles southeast of downtown St. Paul.
Distance:	7 miles of trails available.
Time:	Varies; 12 minutes to an hour or more.
Tread:	All trails are on dirt singletrack, with some loose gravel thrown in to keep you guessing.
Aerobic level:	Strenuous.
Technical difficulty:	Levels 3 to 5.
Hazards:	Loose rocks; steep descents with sharp turns; super-bumpy cross trails on ski runs.
Highlights:	Spectacular scenery in the St. Croix Valley; leg-bustin' climbs; hair-raising descents.
Land status:	Afton Alps.
Maps:	USGS Hudson; best maps available at clubhouse at the top of the hill.
Access:	Exit I–94 at Manning Avenue and go south 7 miles to 70th Street (County Road 20). Head east 3.5 miles to the entrance to Afton Alps Golf Course. Park at the clubhouse and go inside to pay the $6 fee and get a trail map.

Notes on the trail: If you're looking for a workout, head to Afton. This large ski area near the Wisconsin border has 7 miles of loops of varying difficulty in a scenic, uncrowded setting. Most of the trails will test both your climbing and descending skills since the trailhead and clubhouse are at the top of the hill. Tread condition is excellent and the routes are challenging. You are treated to choice views of the St. Croix River valley from many locations on the hill, and the fall riding here is tough to beat. Afton also puts on races during the season if you've got the competitive fires burning; check with their office at (651) 436–5391 for details.

The Ride

0.0 Begin riding on north side of clubhouse. Afton uses red and blue poles in the ground to mark the trails. Keep these on your right. Steep climbs, technical sections of singletrack, and rocky climbs all greet you almost immediately after the start. The trail passes in

Afton Alps Ski Area

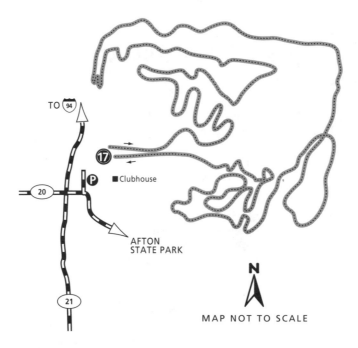

TO 94

17

P ■Clubhouse

20

AFTON
STATE PARK

21

N

MAP NOT TO SCALE

and out of heavily wooded areas and across grassy ski runs: Use caution on some narrow turns and watch speed on the downhills. Beautiful views of the St. Croix River Valley from the top.

1.1 Descend a steep hill and pass a pond on your left, leading to a medium-length climb near bridge loop with loose gravel at the start. Kinda cool to stop and listen to the silence at the base of the hill. Chair lifts rest quietly above you, waiting for the excited activity of winter skiers.

1.4 Enjoy a long, gradual descent with some sections of loose gravel. Take a hard left at the bottom onto a rocky part of the path, then slowly grind back up the hill, following the trail to the clubhouse.

2.1 Back at clubhouse and trailhead.

This loop is just one of many at Afton. Explore the hill on the southern switchback, following the trail and challenge yourself on steep climbs and rocky downhills.

Battle Creek Regional Park

Location:	Between Upper and Lower Afton roads on the eastern fringes of St. Paul.
Distance:	Varies; 1 to 10 miles, depending on your mood.
Time:	10 minutes to 2 hours.
Tread:	Entire loop is on hard-packed singletrack.
Aerobic level:	Moderate + to strenuous.
Technical difficulty:	Levels 3 to 4.
Hazards:	Steep, high-speed downhills; narrow trails with sharp turns; some loose dirt and rocks.

Fun fall riding on the trails at Battle Creek Regional Park.

Battle Creek Regional Park

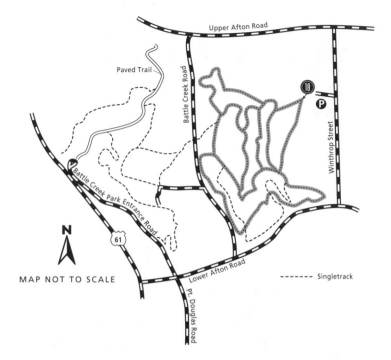

Highlights: Rolling, rollicking trails through thick woods; deer aplenty; lots of different choices of loops to ride.

Land status: Ramsey County.

Maps: USGS St. Paul East; county maps (check Web site for color version: www.co.ramsey.mn.us/parks/parks_trails/map).

Access: From U.S. Highway 61, take Upper or Lower Afton Road to Winthrop Street and proceed north to park entrance. Follow trail signs to fun!

Notes on the trail: Battle Creek has some of the best singletrack riding in the metro area, and it's right up there in the statewide rankings, too. For newer riders, the front side of this park has wide, nontechnical ski trails. You will still go up and down a bit, though, so even those loops require a respectable level of fitness. The really fun stuff is in the woods past the top of the hill. Beautiful, hard-packed singletrack is laced throughout the whole area. Screaming descents, quad-busting climbs, and long, rolling stretches are all there. There are trails all over the place to explore. You'll think you're on a main loop, then another spur trail will shoot off around a curve. It's impossible to resist trying them out. This place really is a playground and it's a blast just riding around discovering new trails. Ramsey County has constructed a new ski trail through the woods that has changed things a little bit. Now there's a nice, rolling, nontechnical trail through most of the park. The county has also worked closely with the Minnesota Off-Road Cyclists Club to build and maintain a few new miles of singletrack. The trails here (and riders like us) have benefited mightily from their efforts. There is more great riding across Battle Creek Road and lots of cool hard-packed trails on top of the bluff dropping down to the paved path.

The Ride

0.0   Head for the hills on wide ski trails, climbing up toward the woods. Pick a path and go. I did a nice little 4-mile loop clockwise around the park. There are numerous side trails all over the place. There's not an official map of these trails, so you'll have to use your built-in compass. Explore like crazy and enjoy steep ups and downs, diverse tread types, and lots of wildlife. Watch for other riders and be ready for greasy conditions after a rain.

Terrace Oaks

Location:	Directly north of I–35E, west of County Road 11 in Burnsville.
Distance:	2.9-mile loop.
Time:	15–25 minutes.
Tread:	Entire loop is mix of gravel and dirt single-track.
Aerobic level:	Moderate +.
Technical difficulty:	Levels 2 to 3, with an expert section of Level 4.
Hazards:	Tight, sharp turns; steep climbs with rocks and roots; fast descents with loose gravel.
Highlights:	All of the above; fun, challenging ride in remote setting within the city; great place to test your bike-handling skills.
Land status:	City of Burnsville.
Maps:	USGS St. Paul SW; map available at trailhead.
Access:	Go north approximately 1 mile from I–35E to Burnsville Parkway. Turn right to park entrance (first right turn). Or take MN Highway 13 east from I–35W to CR 11, then south to Burnsville Parkway. **Note:** Mountain bikes not allowed at west entrance on CR 11; access park only from Parkway entrance.

Notes on the trail: This short trail is another favorite in these parts. Designed by local resident Gary Sjoquist, a tireless mountain bike advocate with a keen eye, Terrace Oaks is a gem in the heart of suburbia. This path shares park space with hikers, and each group has its own designated trail. The mountain bike portion is gnarly, hard-packed singletrack with loads of tight switchback turns through thick woods. Encroaching trees present steady challenges, grazing your handlebars every chance they get. Toward the end of the loop are a couple of long, steep downhills on wider gravel trail that quickly deliver you back at the start. A short detour to a more technical section is available on the back half of the main loop. As its name implies, Terrace Oaks is loaded with mature oaks, along with maple and aspen and a barrage of low-lying shrubbery. It's hard to believe you're surrounded by urban sprawl as you make your way through the park. We are fortunate to have a refuge like this so close to home.

Terrace Oaks

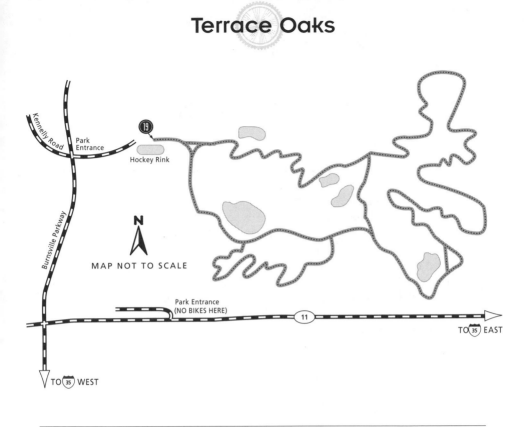

Kennelly Road

Park
Entrance

Hockey Rink

19

Burnsville Parkway

N

MAP NOT TO SCALE

Park Entrance
(NO BIKES HERE)

11

TO 35 EAST

TO 35 WEST

The Ride

0.0   Ride from the trailhead past hockey rink and into the woods. Do not ride on the hiking trail. Stay left at first fork. Signs are posted to lead the way. A couple of short, steep climbs greet you almost immediately, then the trail deposits you onto some tight, twisting turns. Try to keep your bar ends and hands from shaving the bark off passing trees.

1.1   A steep drop takes you quickly through an open area, passing a pond on the left and the cut-off trail on your right. Get ready for a tough hump up another technical climb.

1.4   Long, gradual descent. Be alert for loose gravel. Trail takes a hard left at the top of a small knoll and becomes more rocky. A side trip for experts branches off to the left on the descent. Enjoy some loooong, speedy downhills as the trail makes its way back to the start.

2.9   Back at trailhead. Just getting warmed up? Let's go again!

20

Lebanon Hills Regional Park

Location:	Approximately 0.5 mile southeast of junction of Cliff Road and I–35E in Eagan.
Distance:	2.5-mile loop.
Time:	15–25 minutes.
Tread:	Entire loop is mix of gravel and dirt single-track.
Aerobic level:	Moderate to strenuous.
Technical difficulty:	Levels 2 to 4 + .
Hazards:	Some fast descents on loose gravel; steep climbs on loose, rocky ground.
Highlights:	Sweet, sweet singletrack section rambling through dense forest; challenging climbs; lots of wildlife.
Land status:	Dakota County Parks.
Maps:	USGS St. Paul SW; map at trailhead.
Access:	Go east on Cliff Road 0.5 mile from I–35E to Johnny Cake Ridge Road. Turn right for another 0.5 mile to park entrance.

Notes on the trail: Here's another short loop that is so much fun, most people just keep doing laps. There's enough of a climb in loose gravel at the start to warm you up, then an exhilarating descent. Less than a mile into the ride the trail turns into gorgeous hard-packed singletrack that winds around in the woods. Treat yourself to this ride especially in the fall. A tough expert section is also available if you're up for it. The climbs are steep enough to test your mettle, and several screaming descents balance it out. Before you know it, you're back at the trailhead and too revved up to stop. Multiple trips are the order for this trail. The dedicated efforts of the folks at Minnesota Off-Road Cyclists have made this trail a new favorite in the metro area. New singletrack—5 miles of it!—is being built and will be available by the time you read this. Don't miss it. Keep updated by checking their Web site at www.morcmtb.org.

Lebanon Hills Regional Park

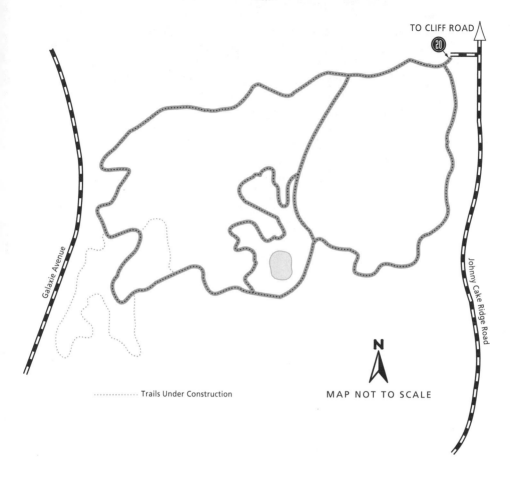

TO CLIFF ROAD

20

Galaxie Avenue

Johnny Cake Ridge Road

N

.... Trails Under Construction

MAP NOT TO SCALE

The Ride

0.0 Begin riding this counterclockwise loop at the west end of the parking area. Trail starts out wide and gravelly, heading up a medium climb. A spur to the left sneaks through the woods for a shorter loop. *Do not ride on the hiking trails. All mountain bike routes are clearly marked.*

0.2 Here's your chance to take a left on this trail for a shorter loop, but keep going straight for maximum fun. Enjoy a long, sweeping downhill with some rocks before passing through an open area to the next junction.

0.71 Junction with hiking trail. Follow the MORC sign into the woods on curvy singletrack. This is great stuff!

1.0 Cross one hiking trail and then arrive at a T intersection. Hang a left, heading up two good climbs with some loose gravel. Reward yourself with a nice descent after the grind up.

1.6 Junction with the expert trail cut-off. This trail is for you if you fancy yourself a mountain bike stud or studette. It's 1.25 miles long, 2 feet wide or less, with over forty log and rock crossings, some of which are 2+ feet high. A great playground to test your technical skills and crash-landing techniques. For this ride, we'll pass on the carnage and continue on to the right. The ensuing downhill has steep sides and a couple of banked turns.

1.8 Ride around a scenic pond to your left and begin gradual climb back to the start.

2.5 Back at trailhead already. Gotta take another lap.

Elm Creek Park Reserve

Location:	3 miles north of the bedlam at the I–494/I–94 interchange.
Distance:	4.4-mile loop.
Time:	15–30 minutes.
Tread:	1 mile paved trail; 4 miles dirt and grass single and doubletrack.
Aerobic level:	Easy.
Technical difficulty:	Levels 1 to 2.
Hazards:	Virtually none. Some bumpy sections keep you guessing, and the handsome scenery tends to avert your eyes from the trail.
Highlights:	Great beginner loop in Hennepin County's largest park; fun paved path and nature center available for diversions from the dirt; lots of wildlife.
Land status:	Hennepin Parks.
Maps:	USGS Anoka; park maps available at visitor center.
Access:	From U.S. Highway 169 and I–94, go north approximately 2 miles to County Road 81. Turn left and take CR 81 for 2.5 miles to Territorial Road. Go right to the park entrance. There is a $4 daily fee.

Notes on the trail: Elm Creek is a gorgeous park, and its bike trails are perfect for new riders. The best time to go is for an early morning cruise through the woods and near the lake. The land and water habitats bring out an abundance of wildlife, and a slow ride through the wetland area of Mud Lake will take you close to herons, ducks, geese, deer, and more. The mountain bike mileage here is wonderful, except for a short stretch of really bumpy trail in taller grass on the north end of the park. If you want to skip the ugly stuff, there are miles of easy paved path to bail out on.

The Ride

0.0 Trailhead at visitor center. Follow signs behind building onto the

Elm Creek Park Reserve

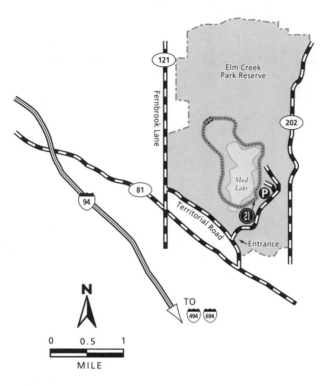

path. Fabulous scenery right off the bat. After an initial glide downhill, enjoy the sights and sounds of the wetland area filtering into Mud Lake. A wooden boardwalk carries you to dry land on the other side. Get off your bike and walk through here; the place is teeming with waterfowl and other wildlife. I scared off a big blue heron and a flock of mallards in the first 10 feet. Stealthily make your way across and you're sure to see all kinds of critters.

0.75 Great views of Mud Lake at the top of a little climb and an excellent place to watch the sun come up. Cross a paved bike path shortly after and continue on the dirt trail.

1.9 At the top of a short, steep climb, go slightly left on the paved path to continue your clockwise loop. Ride for just a couple of pedal strokes and drop back onto the path, which turns to mostly grass. It's really bumpy through this section. When I ride this trail again, I'll take the paved trail and skip the human jackhammer session. Follow the well-marked trails back to the start.

4.4 Back at trailhead.

There are close to 20 miles of paved bike/hike trails at Elm Creek. Try some out to see more of this wonderful park.

Lake Rebecca Park Reserve

Location:	Approximately 30 miles west of Minneapolis on County Road 50, directly south of small burg of Rockford.
Distance:	3.8-mile loop.
Time:	15–25 minutes.
Tread:	Entire loop is oh-so-sweet packed singletrack.
Aerobic level:	Moderate +.
Technical difficulty:	Levels 2 to 3.
Hazards:	A little loose gravel near bottom of some hills; potential crash at a paved trail crossing.
Highlights:	One of the prettiest rides in the metro area and also one of my favorites, especially in the fall and early in the morning; uncrowded, quiet; excellent trail condition over rolling hills with few technical sections; flying turns, quick descents, challenging climbs; a straight-up ideal mountain bike loop.
Land status:	Hennepin Parks.
Maps:	USGS Rockford; park map available from main office or entrance station.
Access:	From Minneapolis, take MN Highway 55 west to CR 50 at the outskirts of Rockford; turn left and follow road to park entrance. Pay $4 daily fee and follow signs to mountain bike trailhead.

Notes on the trail: This is one of my favorite rides in the whole state. The trail is excellent, and the rolling hills and woods are just plain beautiful. You will pass through deep woods, open meadows, and along the shores of a quiet lake. There are quick descents and climbs that make you sweat. The views of Lake Rebecca and Rockford could go on a postcard, and there are several great spots along the way for picnics or rest stops. In addition to the dirt, there are some fun paved trails winding around other areas of the park. What more can you ask for?

Lake Rebecca Park Reserve

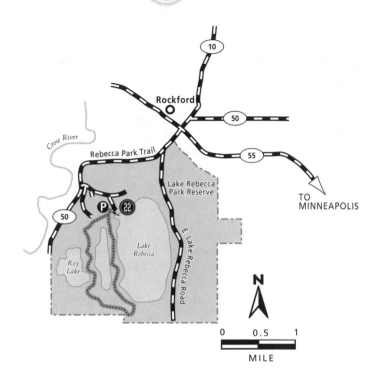

The Ride

0.0 Trail begins at south end of parking/boat ramp area. Phone available at start. Enjoy a nice warm-up climb through dense woods. Great views of open meadow and nearby ponds.

0.92 Cross paved bike path here and stretch your legs on another good hill. At the top, stop and enjoy a fantastic view of Lake Rebecca (here's to ya, Bec!) and the "skyline" of Rockford: just a couple of water towers. Great spot for a picnic.

1.8 Pick up some speed on a long downhill but *beware:* You will cross the paved path again quickly; so use caution to avoid plowing someone over. Continue on the dirt trail over more rolling and heavily wooded terrain.

3.8 Back at trailhead. Can you resist taking another lap? Or how about the 6.5 miles of paved trail? Enjoy!

LRT Trail South

Location:	Trailhead is 0.5 mile south of MN Highway 5 on County Road 4 at the junction with Scenic Heights Road in Eden Prairie.
Distance:	9-mile out and back trail.
Time:	45–60 minutes.
Tread:	Entire ride is on hard-packed limestone path.
Aerobic level:	Easy.
Technical difficulty:	Level 1.
Hazards:	Use caution when crossing roads.
Highlights:	Excellent cruise on old rail line with nice views of the river valley; gradual descent on way down, a little push on the way back; perfect route for all abilities.
Land status:	Hennepin Parks.
Maps:	USGS Shakopee, Eden Prairie; Hennepin Parks offers a convenient map of these trails.
Access:	Start at Eden Prairie Road (CR 4) and Scenic Heights Road and ride southwest on the wide gravel trail.

Notes on the trail: Here ya go: long, straight, flat, and no traffic. Just point your bike down the trail and ride. This is just a portion of the entire trail, but I think this end of it is the best. Soon after you start your ride, you'll enter the edge of the bluffs along the Minnesota River. This area has been developed (destroyed) almost endlessly for many years and has lost much of its original beauty, but it's still a scenic trip toward the river valley. The crushed limestone trail presents no obstacles, and there's not a single hill unless you count the gentle uphill grade on the return trip. It is also easy to access Ride 24 and the State Corridor Trail via MN Highway 41 through Chaska.

The Ride

0.0 Ride west from the trailhead, passing right through the exclusive Bearpath neighborhood.

LRT Trail South

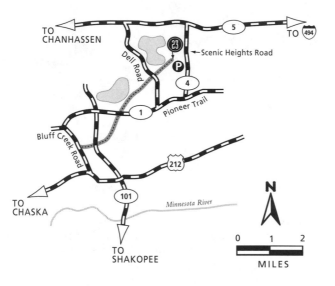

2.0 Skirt southern shores of Lake Riley and carefully cross Pioneer Trail.

3.2 Cross over MN Highway 101 and Bluff Creek. Bluff Creek Road is a fun road for a side trip, with a steep grade and winding curves, but only go for it during off-traffic hours.

4.5 Trail ends at MN Highway 212. You can continue into Chaska along the highway (wide shoulders) for a snack or just head back. Connecting to CR 11 in Chaska will send you out to the LRT North Trail.

9.0 Back at trailhead.

Minnesota Valley State Trail (Eastern Terminus)

Location:	Trail starts at Memorial Park on MN Highway 101 directly east of Shakopee.
Distance:	9.4 miles out and back.
Time:	40–60 minutes.
Tread:	All 9+ miles are on paved bike trail.
Aerobic level:	Easy.
Technical difficulty:	Level 1.
Hazards:	Two sharp turns to watch for oncoming riders; trail will flood after heavy rain.
Highlights:	Easy terrain along scenic river trail; nice trail to cruise and view wildlife.
Land status:	U.S. Fish and Wildlife Service; City of Shakopee.
Maps:	USGS Shakopee; refuge maps (available at refuge headquarters).
Access:	Start at Memorial Park just east of Shakopee. Ride to northeast end of park and cross a short bridge onto the paved trail.

Notes on the trail: Yep, this is a paved trail. I included it because of its location and to give you a head's-up for what is to come. Being on pavement, there are no technical worries on this trail, and mountain bike purists might shy away, but it's a pretty fun ride. The trail winds along close to the Minnesota River and near the original downtown area of Shakopee. (Much of the life has left the old Main Street after the invasion of the dreaded strip malls out on U.S. Highway 169.) At the turnaround point, there is access to the State Corridor Trail and the St. Lawrence rides. As mentioned previously, the state trail is planned to continue through Shakopee and on down the river valley. Stay alert for major changes (not necessarily good ones) if that happens.

Minnesota Valley State Trail

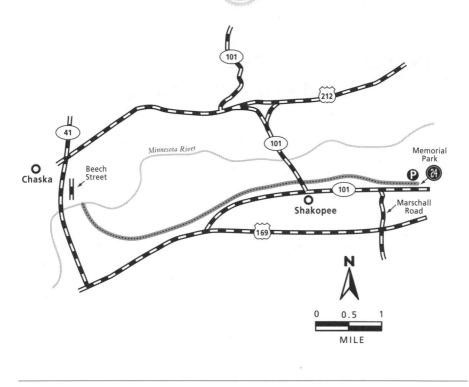

The Ride

0.0   Trailhead. Ride across the bridge and head west on paved trail. You will pass through an RV campground shortly after the start. Be careful not to plow someone down or get squashed by a camper. Continue riding past downtown Shakopee, dropping down through lower river flats and back up onto higher ground with nice views of the valley.

4.7   This is where an old swing bridge waited to whisk you to the other side of the river and on into Chaska. It is long gone now and your ride west ends abruptly here. We hope to see a new bridge built soon. The main stretch of the State Trail shoots off here and offers a lot of miles if you're up to it. It continues clear to Belle Plaine, and a planned spur will be available following MN Highway 41 for access to Chaska. For today, turn around and head back to Shakopee.

9.4   Back at trailhead.

Minnesota Valley—Wilkie Trail

Location:	1 mile west of U.S. Highway 169 on MN Highway 101, south side of Minnesota River.
Distance:	5.2-mile out and back trail.
Time:	20–25 minutes.
Tread:	Mix of double- and singletrack.
Aerobic level:	Easy +.
Technical difficulty:	Levels 1 to 2.
Hazards:	Perpetual bumps on grassy portions of trail; hidden ruts to toss you over your bars.
Highlights:	Flat terrain good for beginners or an easy ride along the river; wildlife aplenty; uncrowded; this trail ranks pretty low on the fun meter.
Land status:	U.S. Fish and Wildlife Service.
Maps:	USGS Eden Prairie; park brochures available at refuge office and (maybe) at trailhead.
Access:	Go west from US 169 on MN 101 through one stoplight, then turn right on narrow gravel road at REFUSE sign.

Notes on the trail: This trail is definitely not one that people generally plan their vacations around, but it's worth checking out if you're in the area. After leaving the initial doubletrack, the trail turns grassy and is laden with hidden bumps and deep ruts. This ride wouldn't even be in this book if it wasn't for the river access and the spur trails that are found in the woods nearby.

Minnesota Valley—Wilkie Trail

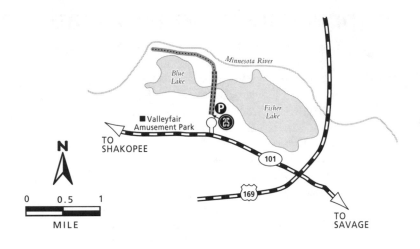

The Ride

0.0   Ride past information kiosk on to gravel doubletrack.

0.75 Reach the riverbank here. Turn left. Trail turns grassy and bumpy. *Do not enter this trail during dates posted on a sign at this point in the trail—herons frequent the area to nest.*

2.5   Trail turns left into the woods, but don't do it, the path fizzles out. You'll have to turn around here and head back.

5.2   Back at trailhead.

Cannon Valley Trail

Location:	Trailhead for this ride is 3 miles south of U.S. Highway 61 on County Road 7, directly south of the Cannon River from the town of Welch.
Distance:	20 miles out and back.
Time:	1.25–1.5 hours, with more miles available.
Tread:	Entire ride is on paved trail.
Aerobic level:	Easy.
Technical difficulty:	Level 1.
Hazards:	Crowded on weekends; use caution when crossing roads.
Highlights:	Excellent ride through high river bluffs; great fall color route; easy access; superb trail conditions.
Land status:	Joint ownership: Red Wing, Cannon Falls, and Goodhue County.
Maps:	USGS Welch; best map is available at pay stations at trailheads.
Access:	This trail can be reached in Cannon Falls, Red Wing, and Welch. Our ride begins at the Welch station, 0.25 mile south of the little town of the same name. Ample parking is available off CR 7 but fills up fast on sunny weekend days.

Notes on the trail: This one's a beauty, even if you're a hard-core mud lover. The Cannon Trail is a great place to spin along, with steep bluffs and rock outcroppings on one side and a meandering river on the other. The riding is spectacular in the fall, and Welch and Red Wing are towns ya just gotta explore. This ride only covers one-half of the entire trail; another 10 miles await to the west to whisk you into Cannon Falls.

The Ride

0.0 Trailhead. Pay $2 daily Wheel Pass (or $10 for the year) and begin riding east toward Red Wing. Shortly after the start you'll ride past Welch Village ski area. Take in the sights of rugged bluffs on both sides of the trail. Great views in the fall.

Cannon Valley Trail

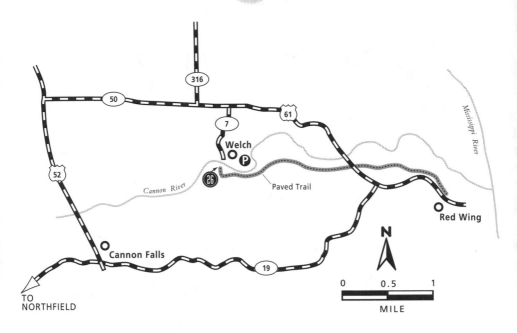

1.5 Ride over Belle Creek on one of many wooden bridges. The next few miles offer good chances to spot all sorts of wildlife both on the ground and in the air.

4.6 Picturesque pasture land to your right with ponds, streams, and cows.

5.1 Pass underneath US 61.

10.0 Trail ends at the outskirts of downtown Red Wing. Signs are posted to take you into this charming town. Plan on spending some time there soaking up the atmosphere. Your return to Welch will be slightly uphill, but it's nothing you can't handle.

20.0 Back at trailhead. Pack up and head over to the general store in Welch to cool down with some ice cream and other goodies.

27

Murphy-Hanrehan Park

Location:	3 miles east of Prior Lake at the southern reaches of Savage.
Distance:	5.8-mile loop.
Time:	30–40 minutes.
Tread:	Entire loop is hard-packed singletrack, with some loose gravel thrown in for a little flavor.
Aerobic level:	Strenuous.
Technical difficulty:	Levels 3 to –5.
Hazards:	Loose gravel and rocks on climbs; high-speed downhills over changing terrain; lack of oxygen as you battle gravity on severe steeps.

Singletrack at Murphy-Hanrehan Park.

Murphy-Hanrehan Park

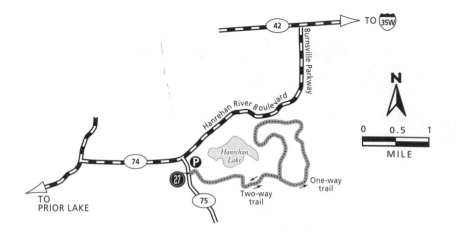

Highlights:	Extremely challenging loop with constant tough climbs and raging descents; quiet ride through scenic, uncrowded park.
Land status:	Hennepin Parks.
Maps:	USGS Orchard Lake; trail map at entrance station.
Access:	From I–35 and County Road 42, go west on CR 42 to Burnsville Parkway. Turn left (south) and go 2 miles to Murphy Lake Road (County Road 75). Turn left and enter park (pay $4 fee at the gate). Phone available at trailhead.

Notes on the trail: Murphy is another top choice among locals and is used by many for serious training. Make no mistake, this trail will make you work. The steep, grueling climbs are matched by the high-speed, technical descents. The loop is short but tough. The tread is excellent, and the trail passes through rolling woodlands with scenic views of adjacent lakes. This area is sensitive to erosion and the trail is only open from August 15 to October 31 to preserve the trails. Check the ride hotline before heading out for updates; trail will close if conditions are bad. Hotline number is (952) 559–6778.

The Ride

0.0   Trailhead. Ride past park building onto singletrack trail. Trail is two-way at the start; use caution. Glide over some rollers and a nice warm-up hill at 0.6 miles.

1.2 Ride past peaceful little pond to right of trail.

1.6 Begin one-way trail here along with a steep descent with loose sand at the bottom, followed by a long, very steep climb. Trail rises in tiers, getting progressively tougher the closer you get to the top. Be ready to granny gear this one. Be rewarded for your effort with a long, fast downhill; be careful. From here on out you will be treated to relentless changes in elevation with steep, technical ups and downs and no chance to enjoy the scenery. This is a serious ride to beef up your hill-climbing skills or punish your riding partner. Come prepared to hammer.

5.8 Back at trailhead.

Buck Hill Ski Area

Location:	17 miles south of downtown Minneapolis on I–35 in Burnsville.
Distance:	Pick your mileage from several different loops.
Time:	20 minutes to 2 + hours.
Tread:	Wide gravel trail and hard-packed singletrack.
Aerobic level:	Moderate + to strenuous.
Technical difficulty:	Levels 3 to 4 +.
Hazards:	Loose gravel on southern switchbacks; tight turns and steep drops on singletrack; some logs and roots on trail.
Highlights:	Fun and challenging trails through the woods with plenty of up and down and multiple loops to choose from.
Land status:	Buck Hill Ski Area.
Maps:	USGS Orchard Lake, or check out the huge map on the wall of the rental building next to the Sports Bucket.
Access:	Trailhead is right at the chalet (next to the Sports Bucket restaurant) and parking area at the base of the hill.

Notes on the trail: Okay, so it's not a huge mountain by any means, but Buck Hill provides some fine riding close to home. The switchback climb up to the summit will stretch your legs on loose gravel and larger rocks, but the fun stuff is in the woods at the northern end of the hill. The trails are marked fairly well, but after awhile I just rode around and explored the numerous loops and spur trails hidden in the trees. The woods trails are maintained well, and the elevation change makes for an all-around great ride. Local bike store Penn Cycle holds BMX and cross-country races here every Thursday starting in May, or you can compete at Erik's Spring Cup. The area is open for riding Tuesdays and Wednesdays from 4:00 to 8:00 P.M. through August. Pick up a $6 trail pass at the Sports Bucket restaurant. Rentals also available. Call Buck for more information at (952) 435–7174.

Buck Hill Ski Area

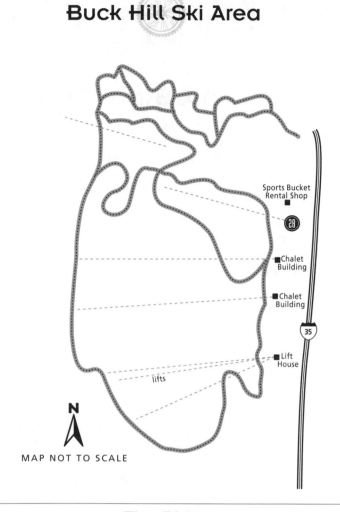

Sports Bucket
Rental Shop ■

28

■ Chalet
Building

■ Chalet
Building

35

■ Lift
House

lifts

N

MAP NOT TO SCALE

The Ride

0.0 Follow wide gravel trail south past the chalet. Trail is loose gravel here and will soon begin to switchback up to the top. Follow path from summit into the woods at the north side of the hill. From here you can choose a number of different loops depending on your ability. Try Don's Descent for some expert-caliber riding, or stay on the fringe of the trees for more moderate rolling terrain.

St. Croix State Park

Location:	15 miles due east of Hinkley and I–35.
Distance:	10.8 miles point to point; 25 total miles available.
Time:	1–1.5 hours.
Tread:	A mix of dirt and grass doubletrack.
Aerobic level:	Easy +.
Technical difficulty:	Levels 1 to 2.
Hazards:	Some loose gravel or sand; relentless pounding from horse tracks; tons of bugs in summer.
Highlights:	Scenic ride through mature hardwood forest; loads of wildlife like black bear, bald eagle, and whitetail deer; close to additional recreation opportunities on the St. Croix River and in the park itself.
Land status:	State of Minnesota.
Maps:	USGS Sandstone South; park maps at entrance station.
Access:	From I–35, head east on MN Highway 48 for 15 miles to the entrance to St. Croix State Park (County Road 22). Go left (south) on CR 22 for 5 miles to the entrance station. A $4 park sticker is required.

Notes on the trail: I'll be honest with you—this wasn't my favorite ride. The park itself is a beautiful place for camping, hiking, canoeing, even biking on the 5 + miles of paved trails. This featured route is a multi-use trail (part of the Willard Munger State Trail), which in theory is a great idea. But you will discover very rapidly that the trail was not initially intended, and is not currently maintained for, riding a bicycle. Horses use this path, too, and while I like a good horse as much as the next guy, the aftermath of their passing bodes ill for a mountain bike. The entire width of the trail, from start to finish, is decorated with inch-deep near circles. I was pounded continuously for the duration of the ride by those infernal equine engravings. I'm all for sharing the trail, but here the horses run the show. It was difficult even to look around with my head vibrating like a melon-shaped jackhammer. To add to the misery, my speed was kept in the single digits to maintain my sanity—not even fast enough to outrun the horseflies. The

St. Croix State Park

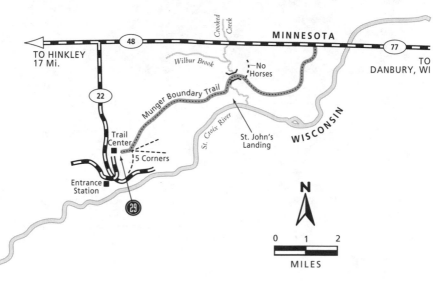

trail continues north from MN 48 way up into Nemadji State Forest and gets worse for any poor soul on a bike. This is snowmobile country, and the trail traces through swamps and bogs and other unfriendly places for fat tires. Don't go that way. The entire portion of the Munger Trail through the park is open for mountain biking, in addition to the paved trails. You may find an area you like at the west end of the park.

I longed for the end of this one soon after it started. And for even more fun, this isn't a loop trail, so if you don't arrange a pick-up at either end, you'll get to do double the distance (bring some aspirin). My intention is not to disparage St. Croix's recreation choices in any way, but the next time I come here, it will be with my hiking boots and tent.

You have been warned.

The Ride

0.0 Begin at the Trail Center area by following the State Trail sign northeast. Go right and ride through a section of deep gravel and a million horse tracks. You will soon arrive at 5-Corners intersection. Turn left here, staying on the far left trail. Trail becomes mostly grassy from here on out.

1.1 Junction with main Munger Boundary Trail. Go right.

2.7 Spur trail to the left with a sign that says NO HORSES. "No Horses" implies a smooth trail, but the designated bike route is straight ahead. Sorry, I know you want to go that way. I feel your pain.

3.6 Pass the spur trail on the right.

The author heading out from the trailhead at St. Croix State Park.

5.7 Small picnic area and backwoods outhouse. Directly south is St. John's Landing, a logging camp in the 1800s and currently a Conservation Corps camp. Stay on the trail as it crosses a wooden bridge over Crooked Creek and climbs up to higher ground.

9.8 Trail merges with a gravel road and follows along its western edge. I immediately jumped onto the road where no horses had been.

10.8 End of ride at MN 48. Ride back to the start if you want to pile up additional miles.

Pillsbury State Forest

Location:	10 miles west of Brainerd and 2.5 miles north of MN Highway 210.
Distance:	27 miles of multi-use trail available.
Time:	1 hour to all day.
Tread:	Mix of gravel forest roads and dirt and grass trail.
Aerobic level:	Moderate, with a few strenuous sections.
Technical difficulty:	Levels 2 to 4.
Hazards:	Steep hills with loose rocks; debris on trail; some taller grass and remnants of passing horses.
Highlights:	Excellent riding on fun trails; cool overlooks; great camping nearby; wildlife loves all the lakes along the trail.
Land status:	State of Minnesota.
Maps:	USGS Pillager; state park maps.
Access:	Go west from Brainerd on MN 210 to Pillager's Forest Road. Turn right and head 3 miles to the parking area.

Notes on the trail: Super-fun riding on rolling trails. Over a dozen small lakes along the way offer a good chance to spot wildlife. The trail doesn't have a straight stretch in it as it winds all over the place on its way north toward Gull Lake. You can ride by an 1886 homestead, a wooden fire tower erected in 1911, and the first forest tree nursery. You may run into some crowding on summer weekends due to the proximity to the many lakes in the area. Be sure to visit the old growth forest just off of County Road 77.

Some different loops to try:

- A fun 10-mile trek east from the trailhead across Little Devil's Ravine, looping around past the old homestead and back down a remote logging trail.
- Double the above mileage by continuing north to Beauty Lake Forest Road and return via the outer snowmobile trail.

Pillsbury State Forest

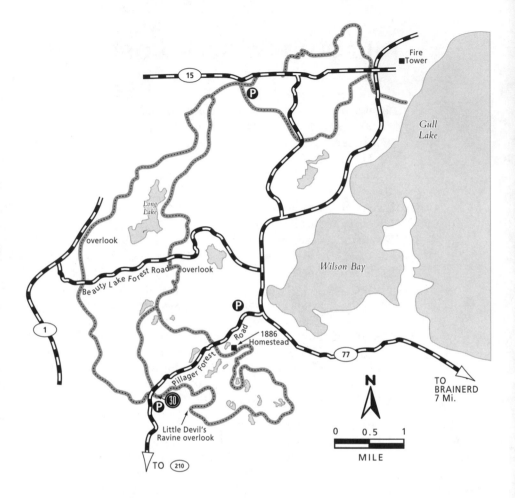

- Take the whole day and journey north and east past the nursery site to the fire tower near Gull Lake. Several forest roads offer alternative loops or bailout options.

Jay Cooke State Park

Location: 3 miles east of Carlton on MN Highway 210.

Distance: 12.7-mile loop.

Time: 1.5–2 hours.

Tread: Hard-packed dirt singletrack with some grassy sections, and a short segment of the paved Munger State Trail.

Aerobic level: Easy, with some moderate stretches in the woods.

Technical difficulty: Levels 1 to 3.

Hazards: An occasional root or loose rock.

Highlights: Excellent tread condition; beautiful scenery; exhilarating ride through deep North Country woods; quiet and uncrowded.

Land status: State of Minnesota. Maps: USGS Esko; state park maps.

Access: Trailhead is located near Jay Cooke park office building off MN 210. From the parking area, ride across the road and onto the singletrack trail. The Forbay Lake Trail will take you in the right direction.

Notes on the trail: This trail is the first in this book that explores the spectacular North Country. The combination of superb trail conditions and the surrounding settings makes the riding up here tough to beat. The coffee-colored St. Louis River rumbles through the park over massive slabs of graywacke and slate, and rock formations of the same jut from the earth all along the ride (the river is only partially visible from the trails, but you can get a close-up view from the swinging bridge adjacent to the park office). This particular region of Minnesota is home to red clay soils, so expect some parts of the trails to have perpetual soggy spots, especially after wet weather. Each of the loops at Jay Cooke is short and is over much too soon, but the journey to reach the loops adds on enough mileage to make this an excellent place to spend a few hours on a fine fall day. The surrounding hardwood forests offer excellent food and cover for a wide variety of wildlife, and your chances are good to spot white-tailed deer, grouse, pileated woodpeckers, and even black bear.

Trailhead at Jay Cooke State Park.

I've hiked this park for years, mostly on the south side of the St. Louis River, and the mountain biking also ranks high on the list of cool things to do in the woods.

The Ride

0.0   Ride from the park office across MN 210 and through the wooden fence to the dirt singletrack. You'll see signs for Forbay Lake Trail; follow this path. The trail is mostly hard-packed dirt, with some grassy spots. Watch for wet and muddy spots along the way.

0.95 Junction 26 with Forbay Lake, a long and narrow offshoot of the St. Louis River constructed for hydroelectric purposes. Take a right and pedal along the banks of the lake. This flat section is largely a two-track service road. The Willard Munger State Trail is directly opposite your current location. Cross the dam and a gravel road back into the woods. Follow the sign labeled FORBAY TO MUNGER TRAIL. When you reach the paved Munger Trail, hang a right.

4.6   Junction with Oak Trail. Turn right, go around the gate, and take the left fork onto a grassy trail. Path quickly morphs into packed

Jay Cooke State Park

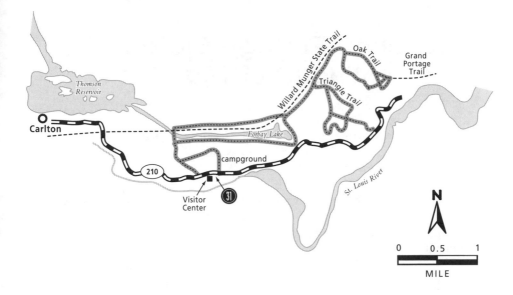

singletrack as it glides gradually downhill through dense stands of aspen and oak, then birch and Norway pine. Turn right at the junction with the Grand Portage trail. Enjoy sweet riding and some nice valley views as the trail winds through thicker stands of pine of both the red and white flavors.

6.7 Emerge back onto the Munger Trail. Go left and ride about a half mile to . . .

7.2 Junction with Triangle Trail. A sign is set off the main route a bit, so be on the lookout. Turn left, cruise down a little descent, and then right at the first fork. This part of the trail hugs the edge of the impressive Hemlock Ravine.

7.9 Another fork; this time go to the left. The right turn option offers some fun expert-level riding with more steeps and more bogs. Gorgeous fall riding on this loop. The aspen, birch, and maple light this area up—very cool stuff. Go left at the next intersection, a four-way junction with a chance to take a short detour to a nice overlook of the valley. Turn left here and ride back to the Munger Trail. There are frequent rollers on this last section, with plenty of gooey spots to contend with. Go left at Munger and ride back to a short bridge at about 11 miles. Turn left around the fence and follow Forbay Lake Trail back to your starting point.

12.7 Back at trailhead. Hopefully you planned ahead and can enjoy the rest of the day camping here and exploring some of the other trails.

Savanna Portage State Park, Continental Divide Trail

Location:	17 miles northeast of McGregor, at the end of Aitkin County Road 14.
Distance:	6.8-mile loop.
Time:	45–90 minutes.
Tread:	Mix of grass and dirt doubletrack and wide, hard-packed singletrack.
Aerobic level:	Moderate.
Technical difficulty:	Levels 1 to 3.
Hazards:	Some loose rocks; roots and logs.
Highlights:	Excellent ride through scenic woods; several loops to choose from; nice climb up and great views from ridge along Continental Divide; very quiet in autumn.
Land status:	State of Minnesota.
Maps:	USGS McGregor; state park maps.
Access:	Buy $4 pass at ranger station at park entrance and follow gravel road to the boat ramp parking area. Begin this loop by following the signs for Shumway Trail and Bog Boardwalk.

Notes on the trail: Great ride starting with a fun trip to a northland bog. Come in the fall for an especially quiet ride through the season's colors. Trails are in good shape and offer a variety of tread and terrain types. The climb up to the Divide can be a tough one, but the view from the top is fantastic. If you have really good eyes, you can see the Atlantic Ocean. Plan to linger up here for awhile. Once the trail dumps you out to the dirt road, you have a chance to relax and spin down to the ranger station, where some fun dirt singletrack on the Esker Trail will whisk you back to the trailhead. There are a few hiking trail loops in this section that are off-limits to bikes, so be sure to bring a map and ride on the right trails.

The Ride

0.0 Ride east toward the lake and follow the Shumway Trail sign. Ride along the west (left) side of Lake Shumway past large pines and into the woods. Trail starts out grassy and turns to hard-packed

Savanna Portage State Park

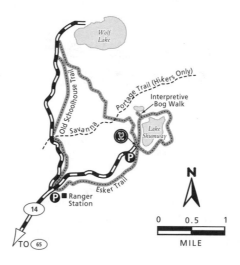

dirt and gravel in the woods. (There is also a trail available that circles around the lake for an additional 2-mile loop.) At about 0.8 miles, take the Bog Boardwalk Trail and ride up to experience this fantastic natural area. Early morning is best, with mist rising from the small lake and floating at the bottoms of the trees. Reach down and gently touch the spongy plant formations. Bogs are the closest thing we have to quicksand—if you stepped into one, it would be no easy task to get back out. You'd for sure lose a shoe or two. After prying yourself away from this wonderful place, head back the way you came to the trailhead and hook over to the Continental Divide Trail at the northwest corner of the parking lot.

1.3 Come to a four-way intersection; follow the middle trail straight ahead, up a long climb to the top of the ridge. Trail is laden with larger rocks embedded into the trail, and numerous roots to negotiate over or around.

2.8 Overlook at the top of the hill. This is the continental divide between the major watersheds of the St. Louis and Mississippi Rivers. Water on one side of the divide follows the Mississippi to the Gulf of Mexico, and on the other side it journeys through the Great Lakes and St. Lawrence Seaway to the Atlantic. From here, the trail takes a steep drop over sketchy terrain to another junction at . . .

3.1 Take a left here on the Old Schoolhouse Trail.

4.3 Junction with a gravel road that leads to the ranger station. Take a left here and cruise down to the park entrance.

5.2 Ride past the entrance station and look for the Esker Trail next to the road. Follow this fun singletrack 1.6 miles to the campground and back to the parking area.

6.8 Back at trailhead.

Washburn Lake Ski Trails, Land O'Lakes State Forest

The Land O'Lakes State Forest consists of nearly 50,000 acres of pine and hardwood species. The last of the virgin red and white pine in this area was removed by logging companies back around 1907. Since then, aspen and birch have regenerated and the big pines are a minority. Mountain biking opportunities include routes on the Woods Lake Snowmobile Trail and Moose River ATV Trail. Numerous resorts and campgrounds within the forest are available for extended stays. Detailed maps can be obtained from the Minnesota DNR and its regional offices.

Location: One-half mile west of MN Highway 6 on County Road 48, approximately 10 miles north of Emily.

Distance: 4.6-mile loop, with options for more.

Time: 30 minutes to 1 hour.

Tread: A mix of wide grassy ski trail and wide dirt ski trail.

Aerobic level: Moderate +.

Technical difficulty: Levels 2 to 3.

Hazards: Many low, wet areas with standing water; roots and loose rocks; lots of horse manure in the parking area.

Highlights: Enough rollers to present a challenge; scenic riding through stands of maple, birch, and aspen.

Land status: State of Minnesota.

Maps: USGS Lower Whitefish Lake; state forest maps; other maps may be available at trailhead.

Access: Traveling west on CR 48, be on the lookout for the Washburn Lake Ski Trail sign and turn right onto the skinny gravel road and parking area. Trail begins at northeast corner of lot.

Notes on the trail: These are ski trails, and they present the usual conditions associated with winter-use trails. For the most part, that means many low areas with mud and water, and more grassy tread than dirt. The

Washburn Lake Ski Trails

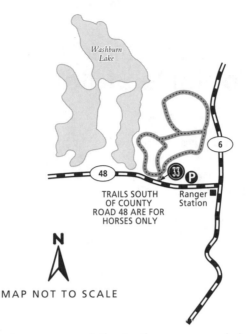

Washburn Lake

48

33

6

P

TRAILS SOUTH
OF COUNTY
ROAD 48 ARE FOR
HORSES ONLY

Ranger
Station

N

MAP NOT TO SCALE

ride is quite scenic however, and the trail goes up and down enough to make the short loop a bit of a challenge. This is a pretty fall ride with an abundance of maple and aspen along the way. The Land O'Lakes State Forest also has miles of ATV and snowmobile trails to explore, but be sure to bring a compass and a lot of water. *Forest staff has recommended the south loop of trails for horses only. Don't ride there.*

The Ride

0.0 Ride past the trailhead sign and onto a wide, grassy trail. Look for the inevitable wet spots right off the bat. Take a right at your first junction and start this loop counterclockwise.

1.5 Junction with a ski shelter adjacent to the trail; go right.

3.1 Another trail junction; continue straight ahead. A left turn will bring you back to the ski shelter.

3.4 Go left at this junction. Go straight if you want an additional 2 + miles.

4.3 Turn left here and then make an immediate right to return to the trailhead.

4.6 Back at trailhead.

Cut Lake Trail,
Foothills State Forest

Foothills State Forest covers almost 45,000 acres of land that was logged to oblivion and abandoned. Similar to neighboring forests, Foothills consists of mixed hardwood and conifer species. Mountain bikes can utilize several snowmobile trails in the area in addition to the ski trails.

Location:	10 miles west of Pine River on County Road 2 in Foothills State Forest.
Distance:	4.2-mile loop.
Time:	45 minutes to 1 hour.
Tread:	Grass and dirt doubletrack and wide single-track.
Aerobic level:	Moderate.
Technical difficulty:	Levels 2 to 3.
Hazards:	Some low, wet areas; some loose rocks.
Highlights:	Great fall ride; longer loop options past Deer Lake and Cut Lake; fun ride through mature pine and hardwood forest.
Land status:	State of Minnesota.
Maps:	USGS Spider Lake; state forest maps; permanent map at trailhead.
Access:	Look closely for the entrance to the trail from CR 2. Begin this loop on the trail heading due north, adjacent to the posted map.

Notes on the trail: This loop is also on ski trails, but these are in better condition than others in the area. It's a very scenic ride through deep hardwood forest. Several loop options are available for different mileages. This loop is short, but once again, the wet conditions mixed with significant bumps make for a jarring ride. You are unlikely to see any living things walking (or riding) out here, and this is another gorgeous place to be in the fall.

Cut Lake Trail

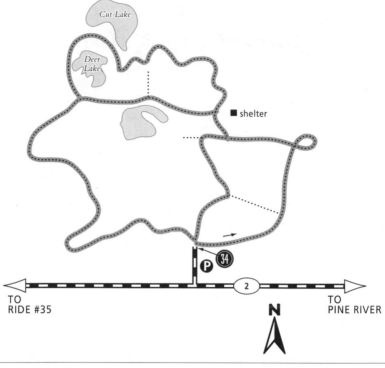

TO
RIDE #35

2

TO
PINE RIVER

N

The Ride

0.0 Ride north from the parking area and take a right at the first junction.

0.45 Go left at this junction.

0.69 Take a right here, then a left at the next split. Pass a small shelter and fire pit on your right.

1.2 Take the left fork here. There is a wooden bench here if you want to rest.

1.7 Take the left fork again, following along the north shore of a small unnamed lake on your left.

1.9 Another bench at this junction; go left. Nice views of some small, remote lakes along this stretch.

4.2 Back at trailhead and parking.

Spider Lake Trails

Location:	10 miles west of Pine River on County Road 2 in Foothills State Forest.
Distance:	7.9-mile loop, with several options for more or less mileage.
Time:	50–90 minutes.
Tread:	Mix of grass, hard-packed dirt, gravel road, and loose rocks on wide trail and singletrack.
Aerobic level:	Moderate to strenuous.
Technical difficulty:	Levels 2 to 4.
Hazards:	Loose gravel; roots and logs; some low, wet areas.
Highlights:	Great chance to explore; very quiet; excellent terrain variety for different abilities; lots of remote lakes; wildlife-abundant.
Land status:	State of Minnesota.
Maps:	USGS Spider Lake; state park maps.
Access:	Follow CR 2 west from Pine River for 10 miles and look for the Cut Lake Trailhead parking area on the north side of the road. Park here and look for the trail heading into the woods on the south side of CR 2. There is also access using a logging road about 1.5 miles west of the parking area.

Notes on the trail: These trails aren't marked for mountain bikes, and the ski markers are hard to read in the summer, but don't sweat it. Take a good map and a compass and just ride. The trails wind and twist and turn and have plenty of challenging climbs and gnarly descents. A logging road and snowmobile trail run through the western edge of the trails for a sure way out if you lose your way. I especially enjoyed the little hidden ponds and lakes nestled among this dense hardwood forest. There is plenty of challenge for the experienced rider, and more relaxed riding for folks new to the sport. The following ride description will get you started on the long loop. Numerous ATV trails also intersect the ski trails, so this could easily be a place to play for a good part of a day.

Spider Lake Trails

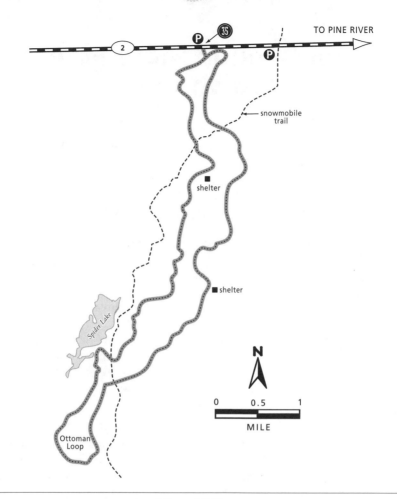

TO PINE RIVER

snowmobile trail

■ shelter

■ shelter

Spider Lake

N

0   0.5   1
MILE

Ottoman Loop

The Ride

0.0 Ride south from the parking area across CR 2. Take a right at the first junction and ride through lowland areas. A couple of good hills will greet you soon, and a steep, rocky descent follows.

3.0 Pass straight through this junction, and continue to follow ski trail markers past a half-dozen pothole lakes and wind around to the eastern shore of Spider Lake. You can shorten your ride here by taking the snowmobile trail to your left. Follow the ski markers back to the northeast; you will eventually return to CR 2 and the parking area.

7.9 Back at trailhead.

36

Paul Bunyan State Forest (South Unit)

Location:	Approximately 8 miles north of Akeley on MN Highway 64.
Distance:	10.6-mile loop.
Time:	1–1.5 hours.
Tread:	Entire loop is gravel and hard-packed forest road.
Aerobic level:	Easy, with some minor hills.
Technical difficulty:	Levels 1 to 2.
Hazards:	Maybe some loose gravel; an occasional vehicle or ATV.
Highlights:	Fun ride on good road through scenic north woods; extremely uncrowded.
Land status:	State of Minnesota.
Maps:	USGS Steamboat Lake; state forest maps.
Access:	From MN 64, turn right at the Martineau Recreation Area Trailhead. I started this loop right here, riding east.

Notes on the trail: This ride is the first ride I did on a forest road, as opposed to an actual trail. Most of the road loops up here are longer in mileage, but the roads are in such good condition they allow you to spin along and soak in the solitude of the North Country. There is virtually no traffic, and the roads curve around lakes and over rolling hills to make for a fine mountain bike experience. There are many miles of road and trail loops in the forest—if you have several days to spare you might be able to hit most of them. This trail also provides access to the paved Paul Bunyan State Trail. Also nearby is Itasca State Park and the headwaters of the mighty Mississippi. Nearby towns of Bemidji and Walker are good sources of inside information on the best trails.

The Ride

0.0 Ride east from the trailhead and MN 64 on the narrow road over some small rollers through thick hardwood forest. Road has some

Paul Bunyan State Forest

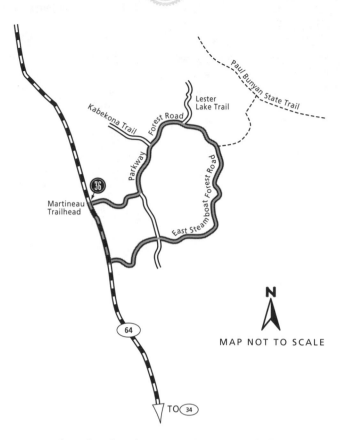

Kabekona Trail

Lester Lake Trail

Forest Road

Parkway Forest Road

Paul Bunyan State Trail

East Steamboat Forest Road

36

Martineau Trailhead

N

64

MAP NOT TO SCALE

TO 34

loose gravel and a few larger rocks to watch for, but overall is in excellent condition.

1.2 Junction with Parkway Forest Road; go left. You'll pass numerous spur trails that snake off into the woods that might be too hard to resist. Go ahead and check 'em out, but remember your way back.

2.8 Pass junction with the Kabekona Trail, which winds back west to MN 64. Sprawling stands of birch mixed with red and white pine line the road through this section. It's a great place to wander into the woods and just sit still.

4.0 Pass junction with Lester Lake Trail. This trail also heads back in the direction of MN 64 and also up toward County Road 39 and Kabekona Lake. Lean to the right at the next fork you come to— you are now riding on the East Steamboat Forest Road. A huge pile of dirt sits on the left, remnants from past gravel operations. There are a couple of snowmobile trails leading out from here, but remember, winter-use trails in the summer are risky at best. Many of them travel through swamps or other unfriendly locales that don't like bikes.

5.6 Pass spur trail to the left that leads out to the Paul Bunyan State Trail and MN Highway 200.

7.3 Stretch your legs on a long, relatively steep hill.

9.1 Four-way junction with the Parkway Forest Road; continue straight ahead.

10.6 Junction with MN 64. You can head back north to the start of this loop or ride across the road for more great trails.

Lake Bemidji State Park

Location:	Approximately 4 miles northeast of Bemidji on County Road 20.
Distance:	4.7-mile loop.
Time:	30–60 minutes.
Tread:	A mix of wide dirt and grass singletrack.
Aerobic level:	Moderate +.
Technical difficulty:	Levels 2 to 3.
Hazards:	Possible collision with a hiker (ride smart); perhaps a log or root to ride over.
Highlights:	Excellent opportunities for wildlife viewing (loons, black bear, deer, coyote); great beginner loop with some climbs for the intermediate rider; access to the especially scenic Bog Walk (no bikes!).
Land status:	State of Minnesota.
Maps:	USGS Turtle River; state park maps.
Access:	Travel north from Bemidji on County Road 21 for 4 miles, then east on Birchmont Beach Drive (CR 20) for 1.5 miles. Park entrance is on south side of CR 20. Trailhead is near the campground. Follow the entrance road back across the highway to begin the loop.

Notes on the trail: Lake Bemidji offers excellent intermediate riding through the heart of Minnesota's matchless north woods. The loop winds past aged pine stands and through dense hardwood forests of maple, oak, and birch. Wildlife abounds in the form of beaver, deer, owls, coyotes, and black bear. Ride quietly and you're sure to see a critter or two. The trail's rolling hills increase the fun factor, and a few steeper climbs will push your heart rate up to higher numbers. Plan extra time to enjoy the Bog Walk—it's a short side trip that will need plenty of time to soak in the solitude.

Check with the excellent staff at Home Place Bike and Ski on Paul Bunyan Drive for inside information on riding in the area. Enjoy great eats in town at several local grills like Slim's and T'Juan's. There is plenty of camping available at the park, which also features hiking, swimming, and picnic areas.

Lake Bemidji State Park

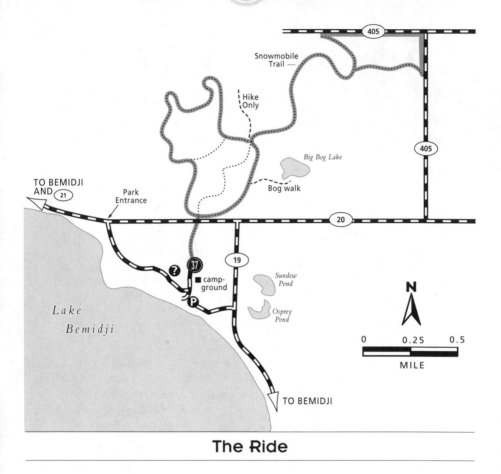

The Ride

0.0 Ride north from the campground, crossing CR 20. Take a left after crossing the road, winding up and down gradual hills.

0.7 Go left at this junction. A long, raging downhill awaits, which is well-maintained for a worry-free descent. Prepare for a sharp right turn at the bottom and a long climb back up the other side. (The wetland area near the bottom of the hill is a great place to spot deer.)

3.0 Take a left at this junction.

3.2 Arrive at a five-way intersection. Here you can choose between several different loops. An immediate left is for hikers only. The next trail to your left is used as a snowmobile trail, which also crosses here to the right. Take a right to get back quickly to the trailhead, or a left to get extra miles in on the snowmobile trail. We'll go straight ahead here. In just over 2 miles, you'll reach the split for the Bog Walk Trail. Be sure to head down there, dismount, and stroll along this walkway to view the extra scenic sights of a northland bog. Then head back to the main trail and ride south to CR 20 and back to the campground.

4.7 Back at trailhead.

Movil Maze Trails

Location:	8 miles north of Bemidji on Wildwood Road, north of U.S. Highway 71.
Distance:	Your choice: 6.5 miles on outer loop or a day's worth of riding on other trails.
Time:	90 minutes to all day.
Tread:	Mix of dirt singletrack and grassy ski trails.
Aerobic level:	Moderate to strenuous.
Technical difficulty:	Levels 3 to 4.
Hazards:	Some muddy sections; roots and assorted debris on trail; easy to lose your way.
Highlights:	Great place to explore; nice views of Movil Lake; rolling ride through scenic hardwood forest.
Land status:	Beltrami County.
Maps:	USGS Bemidji East; best map is ski trail map. Pick one up at Home Place Bike and Ski Shop in Bemidji.
Access:	From Bemidji, head north on US 71 and take a left on Wildwood Road. Look for ski trail signs to reach trailhead.

Notes on the trail: Movil is a fun place to play, but it may be the last place you ride your bike. The Maze is true to its name, with trails splitting off in all directions every time you turn around. Break out your compass and bring along the ski trail map to avoid having to call the air rescue team. You'll run into the usual muddy sections and softer parts of trails associated with ski areas. I'm not a big fan of riding on grass, but overall trail condition is pretty good. With so many offshoot trails, it's just fun to ride around in the woods. Plan on checking in with the staff at Home Place Bike and Ski Shop on Paul Bunyan Drive or other local outdoor shops for the inside scoop on the trails.

The Ride

0.0 From the parking lot, just pick a trail and start riding. Orange markers indicate snowmobile trails, and blue diamonds are ski

Movil Maze Trails

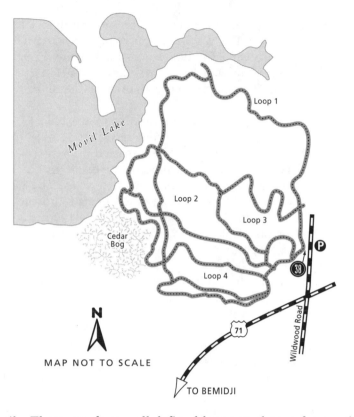

trails. There are four well-defined loops to choose from, with the previously mentioned spur trails laced throughout the remainder of the area. There are nice views of Movil Lake on the outer loop, and you get to ride by a cedar bog, which is always pretty cool. Expect to climb some good hills and enjoy equally nice descents.

Chippewa National Forest Trails

Minnesota is a pretty cool place to live, and a few of the major reasons why are spread across the northern chunk of the state. The Chippewa National Forest offers over 1.5 million acres of northland nirvana. Originally known as Minnesota National Forest, its name was changed to honor its earliest inhabitants. The Chippewa was the first national forest established east of the Mississippi River.

Take a look at a map of the Chippewa: a lot of it is blue. Over 700 lakes, 920 miles of streams, and 150,000 acres of wetland cover the area. Surrounding the lakes and chasing the streams is an immense stand of stately woodland. Some of the residents include aspen, birch, maple, balsam, oak, and elm, but the grandaddies are the majestic pines. The Chippewa has several pockets of virgin red and white pine forests that were spared from the logging scourge of the early 1900s. The Lost Forty area is one place to experience the forests of old, and one you won't soon forget. Thanks to a mapping blunder, this area was shown to be under water, and the mighty pines escaped the saw. Today you can amble among giants in this primeval forest, shrouded in age but radiating with spirit. Nearly 400 years old and 50 inches around, the pines stand proud and, along with their younger aspen neighbors (just sprites at sixty-five years old) provide critical habitat for bald eagles, woodpeckers, weasels, deer, and many other species of wildlife. The Ten Section area and East Lake also offer an opportunity to visit more of these unique sites.

Water activities tend to dominate the Chippewa scene in the form of fishing, canoeing and boating, swimming, and waterskiing. Twenty-six campgrounds can give you a break from the race, and over 400 dispersed campsites allow you to pull out of the race altogether. One hundred sixty miles of trails laced throughout the forest bring you deep into the heart of the Chippewa, be it with boots on your feet or a bike under your bottom. The Shingobee and Suomi Hills Trails are especially groovy. For us mountain bikers, thousands of miles of forest roads provide years of excuses to skip work and go riding. And winter won't slow you down, either. Try ice fishing, superb cross-country skiing, or sledding. Snowshoeing, winter hiking, and snowmobiling are other favorites.

Always be sure to contact a Forest Service office for current information on trail conditions and other details specific to your activity.

Hanson Lake Loop

Location:	4.2 miles south of MN Highway 200 on MN Highway 371, southeast of Walker.
Distance:	16.4-mile loop.
Time:	1.5–2+ hours.
Tread:	Entire loop is on gravel forest road.
Aerobic level:	Easy to moderate.
Technical difficulty:	Levels 1 to 2.
Hazards:	Some loose gravel and deep sand.
Highlights:	Quiet ride in the woods; chance to see deer and moose; several dispersed campsites nearby; very scenic ride on excellent roadbed.
Land status:	Chippewa National Forest.
Maps:	USGS Webb Lake; national forest maps.
Access:	Traveling south from Walker on MN 371, turn left onto Forest Road 2107, which is directly across from County Road 50. This road is also called Woodtick Trail; signs along the route will remind you of that.

Notes on the trail: The Chippewa has forest roads and old logging paths all over the place, most of which are open to mountain bikes. This loop, like many of its brethren, offers gorgeous northwoods scenery in nearly perfect riding conditions. The loop is fairly long, so you'll want to be prepared for a long stretch in the saddle. A fine dispersed campsite is available at Diamond Lake; put your tent and pack on your back and stay the night. Great fishing can also be had at many of the adjacent lakes. Get a good map and bring a compass; all the different roads and trails coming and going can really mess with your sense of direction.

The Ride

0.0   Ride east from MN 371. Don't turn anywhere just yet.

3.4   Ride past two spur roads (or test your luck and see what's down there).

5.0   Junction with Forest Road 3790; go left.

Another hidden road in Chippewa National Forest.

7.5 Curve to the right here, at the junction with Turtle Lake Township Road 42.

9.4 Turn left at 64th Street and ride west. Several homes are along this road.

11.4 Ride onto pavement for a short while to the junction with FR 3759. Turn left here. You will pass FR 3759B; don't turn there.

15.6 Junction with Woodtick Trail; turn right.

16.4 Back at trailhead at MN 371.

Hanson Lake Loop, Gadbolt Lake Loop

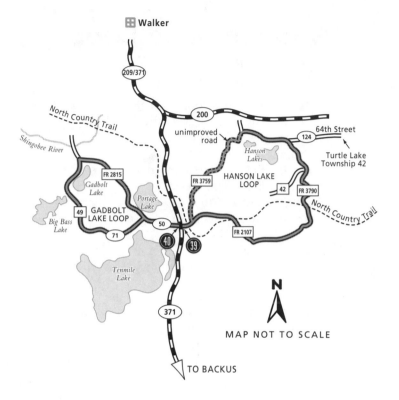

Walker

209/371

200

North Country Trail

Shingobee River

unimproved road

64th Street

124

Turtle Lake Township 42

Hanson Lakes

FR 2815

FR 3759

HANSON LAKE LOOP

Gadbolt Lake

Portage Lake

42

FR 3790

49

GADBOLT LAKE LOOP

North Country Trail

Big Bass Lake

50

71

40

39

FR 2107

Tenmile Lake

N

371

MAP NOT TO SCALE

TO BACKUS

Gadbolt Lake Loop

See map on page 115.

Location: 4.2 miles south of MN Highway 200 on MN Highway 371, southeast of Walker.
Distance: 8.3-mile loop.
Time: 1 hour.
Tread: Entire loop is on gravel forest roads.
Aerobic level: Easy to moderate.
Technical difficulty: Levels 1 to 2.
Hazards: None, except maybe some deep sand and gravel.
Highlights: Fun loop past several scenic lakes; dispersed camping along the way; excellent trail conditions.
Land status: Chippewa National Forest.
Maps: USGS Hackensack; national forest maps.
Access: From MN 371, go west on County Road 50 to the end of the pavement at the split with County Road 71. Ride northwest from here on Forest Road 2815.

Notes on the trail: This is a fun little ride on some superb forest roads. This is a great opportunity to just cruise along and admire the views of some picturesque North Country lakes. There are a couple of dispersed campsites on this route, the better one situated out near Gadbolt Lake. You may run into a car or two near the boat ramps and in the residential area, but overall this is a nice, quiet spin.

The Ride

0.0 Ride onto the gravel road and head northwest. Nice views of Portage Lake on your right. Road is in perfect shape here—smooth and wide and there's no traffic.

2.8 Junction with Township Road 49 (Bachelor Road). You'll pass a boat ramp and nice views of Big Bass Lake to the west.

5.9 Go left at this junction with CR 71. Great views of Tenmile Lake off to the right. Near the end of this loop you'll ride into a residential lake community; watch for a few more vehicles.

8.3 Back at trailhead and junction with CR 50.

Kenogama Trail

Location:	Between Blackduck and Cass Lake on MN Highway 39, 8 miles north of U.S. Highway 2.
Distance:	14.6-mile loop.
Time:	Approximately 2 hours.
Tread:	Entire loop is hard-packed and loose gravel forest road.
Aerobic level:	Easy to moderate.
Technical difficulty:	Levels 1 to 2.
Hazards:	Some loose gravel.
Highlights:	Excellent road conditions; remote, quiet surroundings; good chance to see wildlife.
Land status:	Chippewa National Forest.
Maps:	USGS Pennington; national forest maps.
Access:	Going north, turn right from MN 39 onto Forest Road 2172, just north of the tiny town of Pennington. Ride east on the gravel road.

Notes on the trail: The miles on this loop get a little long for a mountain bike, but it's a fun ride. The back half of the loop on Forest Road 2364 is especially cool. To shorten the mileage a bit, you might try just that part of the ride, or start from the campground at Winnie and cruise around wherever you want. Avoid the Tower Lake Trails unless your bike floats, but there are a couple of other forest roads that take off from this loop that would be fun to explore.

The Ride

0.0 Trail begins at junction of MN 39 and FR 2172. Start heading east down a long, straight, flat stretch. Road narrows and is smooth, with hardly any big rocks or washouts. Road will begin to twist as it turns south.

3.4 Junction with FR 2364; continue straight ahead. And I mean straight, and flat, and nothing exciting for a good mile and a half. Although this is only 3 miles from a major highway, it feels very remote.

4.0 Pass entrance to Tower Lake Trail System. This is for winter use; explore it if you dare, but a swamp awaits that way.

Kenogama Trail

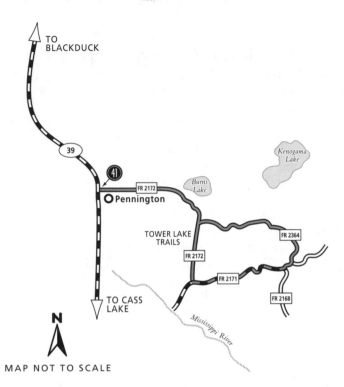

TO
BLACKDUCK

39

41

FR 2172

O Pennington

Burns
Lake

Kenogama
Lake

TOWER LAKE
TRAILS

FR 2364

FR 2172

FR 2171

FR 2168

TO CASS
LAKE

Mississippi River

N

MAP NOT TO SCALE

4.9 Junction with paved Forest Road 2171; turn left (a right will take you back to MN 39). This is another fine piece of road, with no cars in sight and lots of good spots to look for moose or deer or other critters.

7.4 Pass junction with Forest Road 2168. Down that way is the Winnie Campground and the mammoth Lake Winnibigoshish. Keep riding straight on FR 2171 (turns back to gravel here).

7.7 Go left on FR 2364. This is the best part of the loop. The road gets really skinny and big trees arch over the top. It's like a tunnel of fire in the fall. I rode slower through this part so I could give my senses extra time to take in every bit of this beautiful scene. This is vintage northwoods riding.

10.0 You can't see it, but Kenogama Lake is through the trees on your right.

11.1 Back at the junction with FR 2172; go right and head back to the trailhead.

14.6 Back at trailhead at Pennington.

Rabideau Loop

Location:	7 miles south of Blackduck on County Road 39.
Distance:	14.4-mile loop.
Time:	1.25–2 hours.
Tread:	Entire loop is gravel forest road.
Aerobic level:	Easy to moderate.
Technical difficulty:	Levels 1 to 2.
Hazards:	A little loose gravel.
Highlights:	Easy cruising on quiet forest roads; access to two established campgrounds; additional mileage available close by.
Land status:	Chippewa National Forest.
Maps:	USGS Gimmer Lake; national forest maps.
Access:	From CR 39, turn east on Forest Road 2207. Ride begins here.

Notes on the trail: This loop is very similar to the previous Kenogama ride (Ride 41): nontechnical, very quiet forest roads. This ride also has an especially scenic stretch near Rabideau Lake and travels through lowland areas that usually provide wildlife sightings. The ride got a little long for me on the back half. A good move would be to camp at Webster Lake or Benjamin Lake and play on some of the other trails in the area. The Webster Lake loop offers approximately 28 miles of riding attached to this ride.

The Ride

0.0 Ride east on FR 2207's wide, smooth gravel.

1.2 Pass junction with Forest Road 2236. This road offers access to Webster Lake Campground and another 12-mile loop. Keep riding straight ahead on FR 2207.

3.0 Go left on Forest Road 2208. There wasn't a sign marking the road number when I came through here, but there should be a PUBLIC WATER ACCESS sign off to the side of the road. The trail gets much narrower in this section and the woods close in on both sides and shut off light from above. Amazing riding in the fall.

6.0 Junction with Forest Road 2578 at a T intersection; turn right.

Rabideau Loop

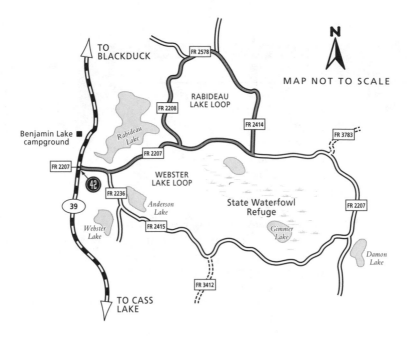

6.8   Another T intersection at Forest Road 2414; go right. Some deeper gravel on this stretch.

10.0   Junction with FR 2207; turn right and head back west.

14.4   Back at trailhead and CR 39.

Lost Forty Loop

Location:	Approximately 30 miles north of Deer River on MN Highway 46.
Distance:	24.3-mile loop.
Time:	3 hours.
Tread:	Gravel and paved forest roads.
Aerobic level:	Moderate.
Technical difficulty:	Level 1.
Hazards:	Loose gravel; vehicle traffic.
Highlights:	Old-growth forest; fantastic interpretive trail along the way; deer and moose sightings.
Land status:	Chippewa National Forest.
Maps:	USGS Dora Lake; national forest maps.
Access:	From MN 46, turn east on County Road 29. Follow CR 29 for 11 miles to Dora Lake Picnic Area. Begin loop by riding north on County Road 26.

Notes on the trail: This is a long loop, but the chance to visit this incredible forest makes it worth the effort. The best part of the ride, and for me the whole point of coming out here, is the opportunity to experience this arboreal marvel. These 300-year-old trees exude an aged strength and authority and beauty that weaken my words to inadequate patter. This is a place to linger and know the peace of the North Country. Keep an eye out for critters like bald eagles and hawks, weasels, pileated woodpeckers, and whitetailed deer. Thanks to a mapping goof in 1882, the Lost Forty (actually 144 acres) was saved, and thankfully all of it is managed to maintain its unique character. Your experience here should carry you along the rest of the loop, but as you near Island Lake on MN 46, the loop becomes a less than epic ride. Back on the return portion on Forest Road 2229, it becomes more woodsy and scenic again and Dora Lake is a welcome sight after a long ride.

The Ride

0.0   Head north on CR 26. At 1.8 miles go left on Forest Road 2240.

2.3   Reach the entrance to the Lost Forty area. Go in there and enjoy.

Lost Forty Loop

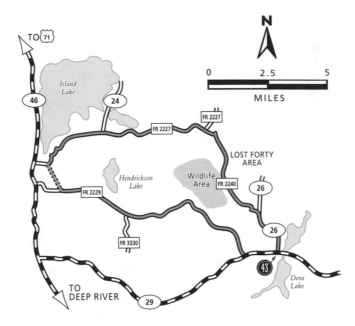

A managed wildlife area to the west of the road provides a better-than-usual chance to see some local furry residents.

3.1   Stay to the left on Forest Road 2227. You'll pass a few spur trails on the long trek toward Island Lake.

7.1   Pass lake homes as the road winds around the south end of Island Lake. At the sharp 90-degree turn before you reach MN 46, keep going straight on the unimproved gravel road.

10.2   Junction with Forest Road 2229; turn left.

22.1   Junction with CR 29; go left back to Dora Lake.

24.3   Back at trailhead.

Simpson Creek Trail

Location: 17 miles northwest of Deer River on MN Highway 46.

Distance: 8-mile loop, with options for more.

Time: 1.5 hours.

Tread: Glorious hard-packed dirt and grass singletrack.

Aerobic level: Moderate.

Technical difficulty: Levels 2 to 3.

Hazards: Larger roots in trail; loose rocks.

Highlights: Gorgeous scenery; excellent trail conditions,
multiple loops to choose from, diverse natural
areas.

Land status: Chippewa National Forest.

Maps: USGS Max; national forest maps.

Access: Trailhead is at junction of MN 46 and County
Road 35.

Notes on the trail: That is one of the best rides in the forest. A layer of needles from the huge red and white pines makes for a soft and silent ride at the start. Farther into the forest, the trail turns first to choice dirt singletrack and then to a mix with grass. I had to keep stopping to listen to the pines whisper their tales. There are many different loops that wind all over, dipping down past an eerie cedar swamp to the picturesque Cut Foot Sioux Lake and providing access to several nice campgrounds. You could spend most of a day playing out here, and the camping areas are beautiful places to round off a great day of riding. For some bonus riding, the Cut Foot Sioux Trail can also be accessed from this same trailhead. You can get on the trail right across the road from the visitor center. The trail parallels CR 35 for a while, then makes a big 18-mile loop around the Cutfoot Experimental Forest.

The Ride

0.0 Ride from the visitor center on the trail at the far northwest corner of the parking lot. Handy maps are usually available from the
kiosk in front of the visitor center. Get one of these for reference

Surreal riding at Simpson Creek, Chippewa National Forest.

at the trail junctions. There are signs posted at most intersections, with a letter that corresponds with the map. This is a great help in planning a route and keeping track of where you are. Trail starts out on wide doubletrack.

0.27 Take a right at this first junction.

0.32 Ride straight across the gravel logging road (Forest Road 2190).

1.1 Go left at Junction N.

1.7 Go right at Junction U.

2.2 Turn left at this unmarked junction. Straight ahead will take you to County Road 33.

2.4 Left at Junction S.

2.9 Go right at Junction T. Cross Simpson Creek and curve around to . . .

3.1 Junction M. Relatively technical here, so use caution. Go right.

3.4 Go left at Junction F, and ride through Junction G. (A picnic area provides a nice rest stop just before reaching Junction F.)

4.2 Continue straight ahead at the five-way Junction J, skirting the shoreline of one of the many bays on Cut Foot Sioux Lake.

Simpson Creek Trail

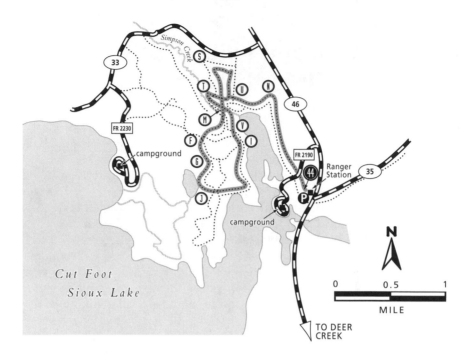

5.3 Turn right at Junction I, ride past Junctions V and M, and cross Simpson Creek again at Junction T.

6.4 Turn right at Junction T, heading back east. Follow either fork past Junction U and retrace your tracks back to the trailhead.

8.0 Back at trailhead.

Suomi Hills Trails
(North Loop)

Location: 16 miles north of Grand Rapids on MN Highway 38.
Distance: 5-mile loop; 21 total miles of trail.
Time: 40–60+ minutes.
Tread: Mix of grass, rock, and dirt singletrack.
Aerobic level: Moderate to difficult.
Technical difficulty: Levels 2 to 4.
Hazards: Steep hills littered with loose rocks; roots in trail; some low, muddy areas.
Highlights: Challenging riding through gorgeous scenery; extremely quiet; stunning fall colors; lots of wildlife.
Land status: Chippewa National Forest.
Maps: USGS Little Bowstring Lake; national forest maps.
Access: Two big signs along MN 38 direct you to the trailheads. This loop uses the northern lot as a starting point.

Notes on the trail: Just getting to Suomi Hills is fun. The other name for MN 38 is the Edge of the Wilderness Scenic Byway, and it is a well-deserved moniker. The picturesque drive in gets you primed for one of the prettiest rides in the forest, and the rolling terrain is more than enough to give your legs a workout. The tread changes offer a medley of grass, dirt, and rocks to put many of your riding skills to good use. There are numerous small lakes on the ride, surrounded by thick stands of maple, basswood, aspen, and birch, with scattered pine thrown in. You're almost sure to see loons and beaver on the lakes, and you may also have some company in the form of coyotes, deer, black bear, or bald eagles. Spruce Island Lake is one highlight of this ride, and there is a cozy little point just off the trail, which is a great spot to take a breather or have a snack. Several

Hidden lake on Suomi Hills Trails.

secluded backcountry campsites offer other options for adventure. Come in the fall and you'll find it hard to leave.

The Ride

0.0 Start riding south on the trail at the southeast corner of the parking lot. Pedal past a stand of towering pines, then push up a long, rocky climb. You are rewarded with an equally long descent past a hidden lake.

0.68 Take the middle path at this confusing intersection. The far left trail will take you past Kremer Lake and to the southern loop in this system. A nice long climb greets you right off the bat.

0.86 Ride straight past the log bench. Plenty of rocks and hidden roots in the trail in this stretch.

1.8 Cross a small wooden bridge.

Suomi Hills Trails

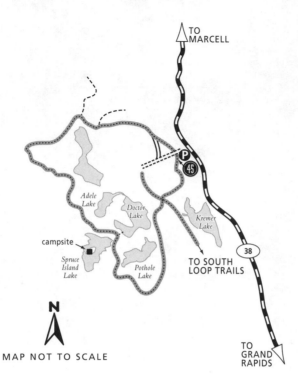

TO
MARCELL

P
45

*Adele
Lake*

*Doctor
Lake*

*Kremer
Lake*

campsite

*Spruce
Island
Lake*

*Pothole
Lake*

TO SOUTH
LOOP TRAILS

38

N

MAP NOT TO SCALE

TO
GRAND
RAPIDS

2.3 Spruce Island Lake appears on your left. Get your camera out. Cross another bridge at the edge of the lake and onto some fun singletrack.

2.6 Follow the fork to the left.

3.5 Long, steep descent. Use caution.

4.2 Go right at this junction.

4.4 Take the path to your right, then go left on dirt forest road.

5.0 Back at trailhead.

Scenic State Park

Location:	7 miles east of Bigfork on County Road 7.
Distance:	4.9-mile loop.
Time:	30 minutes to 1 + hours.
Tread:	Gravel road at start, then singletrack to die for; some pavement at end.
Aerobic level:	Easy to moderate.
Technical difficulty:	Levels 1 to 3.
Hazards:	Scenery is too beautiful to concentrate; an occasional root.
Highlights:	Same as above, plus superb trail conditions and magnificent virgin-pine forest; great new rider loop.
Land status:	State of Minnesota.
Maps:	USGS Bigfork; state park maps.
Access:	From Bigfork, head east 7 miles to County Road 75 and turn left into park. Start from ranger station or trail along lakeshore at northeast corner of Chase Point campground.

Notes on the trail: I'm speechless. I've been reduced to just a shell of my former writer's self attempting to recap this fantastic ride. I believe this could be called the perfect place to ride a mountain bike. The trail starts out with a warm-up on a smooth access road, then climbs gently up to a fire tower lookout. You will wind past immense old-growth pines on a soft pine needle-covered surface, then descend down a short hill with scattered small boulders. Back at the base of the hill, the trail travels through deeper sand and gravel and past a short boardwalk through a hushed northland bog. An additional loop east of the fire tower provides some tougher terrain and an extra couple of miles. Secluded backcountry campsites are tucked in along the shores of Pine Lake—bring your tent for double the fun.

The Ride

0.0 From Chase Point Campground, head to the northeast corner and look for the trail (old, beat up, and cracked pavement). Follow this

Scenic State Park

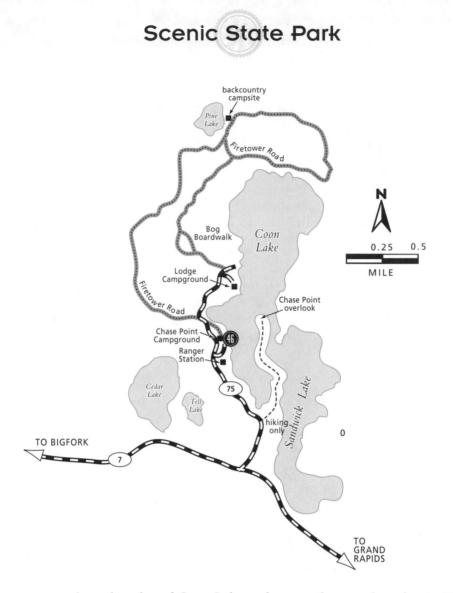

along the edge of Coon Lake and across the paved road onto Fire Tower Road, a smooth gravel doubletrack. Trail gradually rises and you will soon enter dense pine forest.

2.3 At junction with trail for the backcountry campsites and Pine Lake, go right and ride to the fire tower. I tarried for a bit up here, wandering down to the well for some fresh water and checking out the remains of an old ranger cabin. The fire tower itself is open for tours on Saturday afternoons; I missed it when I was here but that would be a pretty cool trip, too. Check with park office for current schedules. When you're ready, take off on the path that heads back southwest. The descent is a blast—rocks and roots on hardpack with just enough of a grade to liven things up.

3.4   Go left at this junction. Trail is now a wider road through deep sand and gravel with lowland to the west.

3.8   Junction with the bog boardwalk. Take the time to check it out; the ancient glaciers left some spectacular sights. Continue on the wide trail and cross the paved road into the lodge campground and take an immediate right, following the roads past the log cabin buildings in the heart of the campground. Ride the paved road back to the initial starting path and back into Chase Point Campground.

4.9   Back at trailhead.

Giants Ridge Ski Area

Location:	5 miles northeast of Biwabik on County Road 138.
Distance:	60 total miles of trail, with many more available nearby.
Time:	Multiple days of fun.
Tread:	Grassy ski trails and some gravel.
Aerobic level:	Easy to strenuous.
Technical difficulty:	Levels 1 to 3.
Hazards:	Hidden rocks or roots; trails may include several wet sections.
Highlights:	60 miles of trails! Excellent selection of loops for all abilities; fantastic views from the top; great rental shop on site with expert staff.
Land status:	Giants Ridge Ski Area.
Maps:	USGS Dewey Lake; best maps available at rental shop on site.
Access:	From Biwabik, follow MN Highway 135 to CR 138 and turn left on CR 138. Follow to ski area, which will appear on your left.

Notes on the trail: The Ridge is another of Minnesota's finer ski areas with great mountain biking in the summer. There are 60 miles of trails at the ski area, and at least that many more in the immediate area. Easy trails with gentle rollers are sprinkled throughout the area, and more experienced riders can challenge themselves on routes with long climbs and white-knuckle descents. The great new Round the Mountain loop will have the whole family grinning, and new construction on the Oslo Trail offers more fantastic views of the surrounding forest. The staff at the rental shop can give you expert advice and set you up with a sweet bike for an epic day of riding.

Here are some of the favorites:

GOLD TRAIL

A 9.3 mile loop that sends you up and down the mountain three times with 1,500 feet of climbing. Nontechnical, but the long climbs will test you. Great fun coming down!

Giants Ridge Ski Area

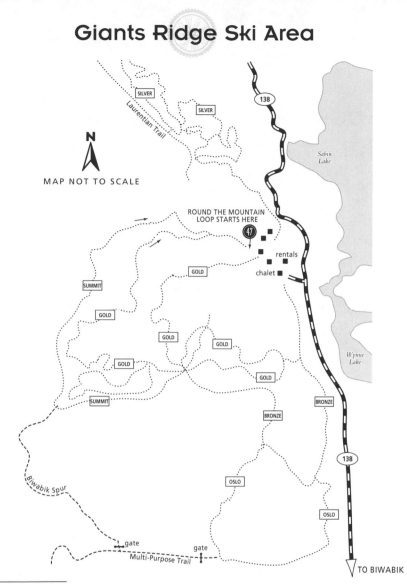

MAP NOT TO SCALE

SILVER

SILVER

Laurentian Trail

138

Sabin Lake

ROUND THE MOUNTAIN
LOOP STARTS HERE

47

rentals

chalet

GOLD

SUMMIT

GOLD

GOLD

GOLD

GOLD

GOLD

GOLD

SUMMIT

BRONZE

BRONZE

Wynne Lake

Biwabik Spur

138

OSLO

OSLO

gate

gate

Multi-Purpose Trail

TO BIWABIK

SILVER TRAIL

One of the most popular loops. This is a 6.2-mile roller coaster on the north edge of the ski area. Lots of short power climbs on a squiggly trail with beautiful views of the neighboring Laurentian Trail.

ROUND THE MOUNTAIN LOOP

More than 13 miles combining five different trails for the consummate mountain bike ride (see official resort map for details). This one has some skinnier, more intimate trails traveling through swamps, woods, and more open country. Excellent chance to spot wildlife in the distinct ecosystems. Several ski shelters along the way are great for rest stops. Bring the kids!

Gooseberry Falls State Park

Location:	Approximately 35 miles north of Duluth on MN Highway 61.
Distance:	6-mile loop (mileage options available).
Time:	50–90 minutes.
Tread:	Mostly grassy ski trails, with some hard-packed dirt.
Aerobic level:	Easy to moderate.
Technical difficulty:	Level 2+, with a few steeper climbs.
Hazards:	Numerous wet mud pits; trail sections may be closed for maintenance.
Highlights:	Typically gorgeous northwoods scenery; non-technical trail; access to several outstanding views of the forest and Lake Superior.
Land status:	State of Minnesota.
Maps:	USGS Castle Danger; state park maps.
Access:	From parking area at Interpretive Center, ride on path through the woods or out the entrance road to MN 61 and make your way to the old visitor center on the west side of the road. Trail begins immediately north of the building. (Recent construction in the area may change this.)

Notes on the trail: You won't be disappointed with the beauty of this park, and the riding is almost as rewarding. Once again, this route travels on ski trails, and past rides have already revealed that tread condition will be less than stellar. Short sections of gooey mud await throughout the ride, some sticky enough to require dismounting and walking through. I did this ride late in the season (October) after a long, rainless stretch, and it was still wet in these spots. Stay far away from this trail after a rain, or bring your hiking boots and sample the epic Superior Hiking Trail.

The back half of the ride is the best, with a super view of the Sawtooth Mountains and substantially better tread. You'll also ride through deeper woods with a couple of fun descents. Glimpses of the big lake add to the fun.

View of Sawtooth Mountains at Gooseberry Falls State Park.

The Ride

0.0 I started mileage at the Interpretive Center. Ride toward US 61 (pass under the road on a bridge), then head north to old visitor center. At north side of building, take second trail from left.

0.4 Ride straight through this four-way intersection. Continue past the next spur trail on the left.

0.6 Arrive at a Y in the trail; go left.

0.8 Take the time to walk down to the bridge over Fifth Falls, an impressive sight where the river tumbles through a deep gorge. Continue on the trail to the next junction.

1.0 Go right here past the DO NOT ENTER sign. These are only for skiers in winter. The trail winds through an area that looks like a birch tree graveyard: Dozens of trees shortened to a fraction of their former height by age or disease or some other malady—kinda creepy. A gradual climb will bring you to a ski shelter and a trail coming from the left. Keep going straight.

1.5 Junction with a snowmobile trail; go straight. Trail works its way to higher ground through more dense stands of pine and carpets

Gooseberry Falls State Park

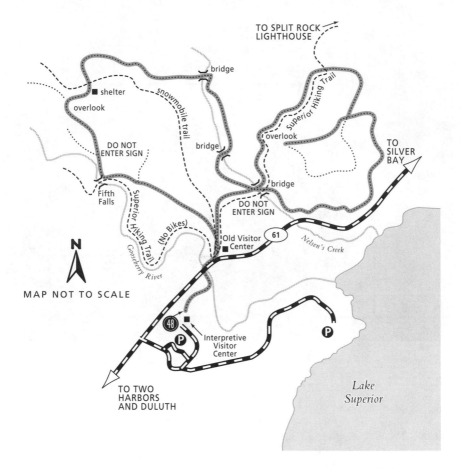

of lichen on the nearby rocks. Look for grouse blending in with the foliage.

2.0 Watch for low spots here. Some of the footbridges may be out as you cross Nelsen's Creek so stay alert.

2.4 Go right after crossing Nelsen's Creek.

2.6 Ride for a short way on the Superior Hiking Trail. It is legal to ride on Superior Hiking Trail only on this section in the park. Pedal up the big hill and past the turnoff left to Split Rock Lighthouse. **Note:** As much as you might want to, don't ride on the hiking trail out of Gooseberry. Beyond here that path is for hikers only. You'll begin to see glimpses of Lake Superior through the trees.

3.2 Take a right at this junction and climb up to a helluva nice view of the Sawtooth Mountains, especially in the fall. Do not forget

Fall riding among the birch at Gooseberry Falls.

your camera! Then go back to the main intersection and head straight through, enjoying a long descent and some rollers through dense pockets of birch and aspen.

4.3 Turn left onto the DO NOT ENTER trail. Nice view of Lake Superior here.

5.3 Arrive at the start of trail and old visitor center.

6.0 Back at trailhead/Interpretive Center.

49

Split Rock Lighthouse State Park

Location:	Approximately 45 miles north of Duluth on MN Highway 61.
Distance:	6.2-mile loop.
Time:	Approximately 1 hour.
Tread:	Mix of hard-packed dirt and grassy ski trail.
Aerobic level:	Easy to moderate.
Technical difficulty:	Levels 1 to 2.
Hazards:	Watch for hikers throughout the loop; numerous mud pits on the trail west of MN 61.
Highlights:	Dazzling scenery, especially near and including Lake Superior; great side trip up Day Hill; a tour at the lighthouse is always interesting.
Land status:	State of Minnesota.
Maps:	USGS Split Rock Point NE; state park maps.
Access:	Enter the park from MN 61. From the park entrance station, follow the road to the Trail Center parking area. Ride past the big picnic shelter adjacent to the lot and onto the paved Little Two Harbors Trail, heading south.

Notes on the trail: This trail is very similar to Ride 48. The shoreline here is spectacular and makes it difficult to keep your eyes on the trail. There are plenty of great views of the lighthouse right off the bat and good tread conditions. When the path continues on the other side of the highway, it becomes a ski/hike/bike trail: grassy and muddy. This is still a fun ride and the forest is inviting, but plan on dismounting a few times if you don't have a high skill level—the many low sections had deep enough mud to bring my bike to a rapid halt. I enjoyed the trail on the lake side of the highway much better.

Be sure to take the climb up to the top of Day Hill (it's rideable if you really go after it). The view from the top is beyond any of my meager words. I didn't come back down for a while. The lighthouse is a bonus for an après-ride activity. If you've never been to the North Shore, plan on spending plenty of time off the bike and in your hiking boots exploring nature's incredible handiwork along the cliffs and shores of Lake Superior.

A secluded bridge on Split Rock Trail.

The Ride

0.0 Ride toward the lake past the big picnic shelter and onto the paved trail. Ride south and west away from the lighthouse. Control your speed and watch for hikers. Trail will eventually turn into a wide gravel path. You'll have a fine view of the lighthouse along the shore near the island, shortly after the beginning of the ride.

0.05 Bear right with the Superior Hiking Club signs. Do not ride beyond this point on the hikers-only portion of Day Hill Trail. A challenging climb will take you closer to the top of Day Hill.

0.20 Don't miss the chance to go left here and up the final stretch to the summit of Day Hill to one of the most dazzling views you'll find of Lake Superior. On a clear day the Apostle Islands and the northern reaches of Wisconsin reveal themselves 50 miles away. Look for the big ore freighters steaming out from Twin Ports. This is truly an awesome sight, and this rock is also a great place to hang around for a picnic or just plain old sittin'.

0.50 Come to a Y in the trail; go right for a short way to MN 61. Cross the road carefully and ride back onto a wide, grassy ski trail. It's real wet through these first sections—feels like a cyclocross trail.

Split Rock Lighthouse State Park

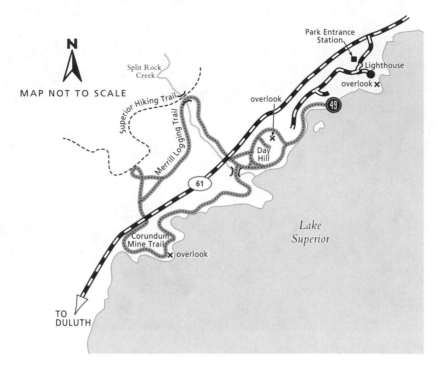

1.3 Pass junction with Superior Hiking Trail. There will be signs labeled MERRILL LOGGING TRAIL. The path will cross a footbridge over a serene segment of Split Rock Creek making its slow journey to the big lake. After crossing the creek, the trail is mostly drier than what you've seen so far, but it is riddled with hidden roots and rocks buried beneath the grass. They're tough to see until you're on top of them; this is a good place to endo if you're not paying attention.

2.7 A fork in the road; go left. (A right turn will take you up a tough climb to a nice overlook.)

3.1 Junction with MN 61. Cross carefully and go right on the weathered pavement. Where the road ends, take a left back onto the Corundum Mine Trail and begin to work your way back toward the lighthouse.

4.4 Take the fork to the right.

5.1 Turn right here and ride to the junction with the Day Hill hiking trail. Turn left at this junction and climb back up to the upper portion of Day Hill, turning right and following the trail back the way you came to the trailhead.

6.2 Back at trailhead.

Superior National Forest Trails

I found myself grinning as I abruptly remembered that I was *working* while I careened down a heavenly slice of singletrack in one of the most beautiful natural settings on the globe. Yep, this day the extraordinary Superior National Forest was my office: a nearly four-million-acre playground in which to conduct the painstaking research (fun) that went into this book.

After those glaciers melted 10,000 years ago, they left behind the lakes, bogs, and craggy rock outcroppings that form this boreal forest, the only one that thrives in the continental United States. Superior National Forest is composed of a backdrop of magnificent pine forest chock full of aspen, birch, maple, and fir, a veritable who's-who of tree species. But try as they might, the trees can't hide the water. The Superior boasts almost a half-million acres of surface water, including over 2,200 miles of warm and cold water streams. The abundance of water and vast woodlands make for excellent wildlife habitat, the most notable being the timber wolf. Northern Minnesota is home to the largest population of wolves in the nation; close to 400 of the seldom-seen symbols of the wild now wander here. Other wildlife that call the Superior home include black bear, whitetailed deer, pine marten, ruffed grouse, loon, bald eagles, and a myriad of other bird species.

Many of the finest mountain bike routes in the state can be found along or near Lake Superior's North Shore. You can ride in the deep woods at Gooseberry or sample miles of wonderful singletrack at Lutsen and Pincushion, all the while taking in stunning views of the big lake. Venture a bit farther inland and you'll find a web of thousands of miles of forest roads and logging paths through the Superior, offering years of riding potential. I planned my riding in this area for the fall of the year, when nature starts to show off. There's nothing quite like the sight of the aged Sawtooth Mountains resplendent in fiery autumn dress. Aspen leaves flutter golden while the maples attempt to outdo them with blazing orange and vivid red. It always seems to take longer to ride up here in the fall because you have to keep stopping to look at another great view. It is truly a spectacular place.

You won't even be lacking things to do once you park your bike. Try canoeing some of those 2,000 miles of streams, or paddle a kayak out on Lake Superior. Fishing in the area is world-class, and hiking in the North Country is tops nationwide. The Superior Hiking Trail brings you close to the very heart of the land, passing waterfalls and cascading streams and traversing canyons and deep northland forests. It's plenty long, too, extending from Duluth all the way to the Canadian border.

When the snow flies, we just change equipment and head back out. More than 400 miles of groomed cross-country ski trails are available in the forest, and if that's not enough, two million acres of woods will get you first tracks almost every time. Lutsen Mountains is a mecca for the downhill ski crowd, and snowshoeing is great fun, too. Again, contact Superior National Forest offices for the latest information. Details can be found in Appendix B.

Big Aspen Trail

Location:	Approximately 11 miles north of Virginia adjacent to U.S. Highway 53.
Distance:	5.8-mile loop (multiple loops available).
Time:	45–75 minutes.
Tread:	Dirt and grass ski trail; gravel road.
Aerobic level:	Moderate +.
Technical difficulty:	Levels 1 to 3.
Hazards:	Several low, wet areas; lots of roots and loose rocks at start.
Highlights:	Excellent fall color loop; rolling terrain through quiet hardwood forest.
Land status:	Superior National Forest.
Maps:	USGS Deer River; national forest maps.
Access:	From US 53, go east on County Road 131. Turn left on County Road 68, and continue straight at the split for County Road 405 to the parking lot and trailhead.

Notes on the trail: Another fun ride with several loop options to choose from. Best time is in the fall when the aspen-heavy forest turns ablaze. Rolling terrain on grassy trails gives you a workout, and there are numerous wet spots to negotiate. This particular ride gives you a sample of grass, dirt, and gravel road all in one loop. Lots of other routes available for more fat tire fun.

The Ride

0.0 Grab a handy map at the trailhead and ride onto the trail right in the middle of the split between Forest Road 256 and Forest Road 257. The trail is littered with embedded rocks, but it's not too tough to negotiate around or over them.

0.8 Take a left at this first junction.

1.4 Junction 9; go right. Each intersection is numbered and has a posted map, which makes it really nice to keep track of where you are out here. The map at the trailhead is an invaluable tool. Grassy doubletrack through this section.

Big Aspen Trail

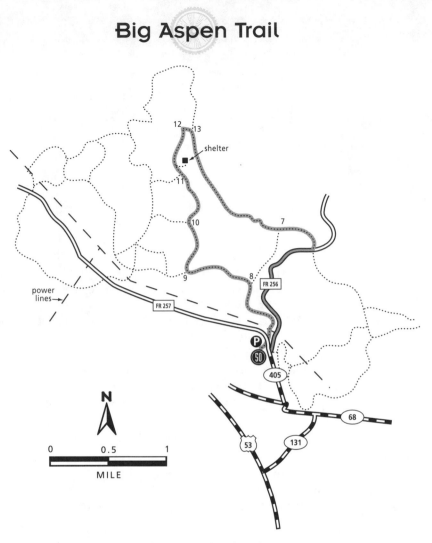

1.9 Junction 10; keep riding straight ahead.

2.4 Junction 11; go right. Ride past the spur trail that leads to a ski shelter. You'll find a long, rocky descent here. Lots of loose rocks threaten to dismount you from your bike, so use caution.

2.8 Junction 12; take a right. Some of the posted maps have fallen victim to knuckle-dragging hunters who found something they could shoot at that wasn't moving, so you might not be able to rely solely on the trail signs. Take another right at Junction 13.

4.1 Junction 7; go left. A right turn here will take you back to your starting trail.

4.6 Junction with FR 256; go right. The trail also continues across the road and loops back to the trailhead if you're hungry for extra mileage.

5.8 Back at trailhead.

51

Lutsen Mountain Bike Park

Location:	90 miles north of Duluth on MN Highway 61.
Distance:	35+ miles of marked trails available.
Time:	Half-hour to multiple days.
Tread:	Grassy, gravel, and dirt single- and double-track.
Aerobic level:	Levels 1 to 5—take your pick.
Technical difficulty:	Easy to strenuous.
Hazards:	Loose rocks; roots and similar debris; mud holes; jaw-dropping scenery.
Highlights:	Same as above, plus superb surroundings, excellent trail maintenance, and great trail variety.
Land status:	Lutsen Mountains.
Maps:	USGS Lutsen; best maps available on site.
Access:	Follow signs for Lutsen from MN 61 on the access road and work your way to the mountain bike building. Purchase a trail pass for $14–$23 (includes lift access), get a map, and ride!

Notes on the trail: Yahoo! This place rocks for mountain biking! Lutsen has it all, from white-knuckle, technical descents to relaxed cruising. Four separate mountains provide an assortment of trails for riders of all abilities, and each trail is numbered and color-coded for easy navigation. Mystery Mountain serves up sensational singletrack riding, rolling through the woods and crossing the falls over the Poplar River. Moose Mountain offers challenging rides that rival some of the epic trails I've ridden in the Rockies: technical riding along the upper ridgeline, 1,100 feet above Lake Superior, snakes around and drops down to the Cascades, an expert rider's playground over rock ledges. Eagle Mountain makes you work up a steep climb, then rewards your efforts going down. The trail on Ullr Mountain has great views of the wetlands above the falls, and there's a good chance to see moose and friends as you gradually climb into the forest. You'll need a trail pass to ride here, even if you don't use the lifts, but it's worth every penny. I like to ride *up* the hills at ski resorts, but the lifts let you get in a whole day of fun. Great campgrounds are available nearby, and Lutsen

Lutsen Mountain Bike Park

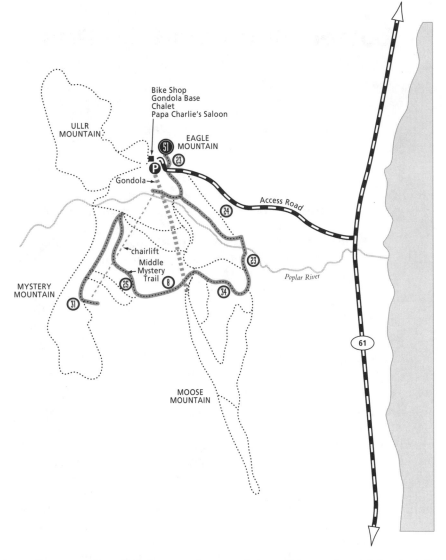

also offers excellent lodging on site, an alpine slide, and good food at the Mountaintop Deli or Papa Charlie's. Forest road riding is almost endless in adjacent national forest areas, and world-class hiking trails make their way through the area as well.

The Ride

This is just one short loop around Mystery Mountain. Sample them all to get the full Lutsen experience.

0.0 Ride across the road from the bike rental shop to trail 23 and glide down a long descent to the Mystery chairlift. Grab a seat and enjoy the easy way up. Be sure to look behind you for beautiful views of Lake Superior and the neighboring mountains. At the top, ride straight ahead and onto trail 31. This is singletrack riding at its finest: hard-packed with scattered rocks to hop over and, if you're here in the fall, views so spectacular it's hard to watch where you're going.

1.1 Merge with trail 25 and ride across the ski slopes and under the chairlift. Trail snakes and twists and rolls to the junction with Middle Mystery Trail. Hang a right here. A few wet sections through this stretch and a touch higher difficulty level. You will soon merge will trail 6 and begin heading downhill.

2.3 Four-way intersection; head straight across on trail 8. (If you turn right here, you can hoot and holler down trail 34 to the challenging ledge rock riding at the Cascades.) Trail 8 drops down a steep, rocky path. Trail is a carpet of loose rocks, and the grade is steep enough to cause you all sorts of grief if you don't pay attention. Use caution.

3.0 Cross over the Poplar River and ride along the river on trail 23 (trail 24 will also lead back to the lodge area).

3.5 Junction with the original trail down from the top. Turn right and push back up the trail you had so much fun coming down at the beginning. It's two-way trail through here, so be alert for oncoming riders.

4.3 Back at trailhead.

Pincushion Mountain Trails

Location:	2 miles north of Grand Marais on the Gunflint Trail (Cook County Road 12).
Distance:	4.6-mile loop.
Time:	45 minutes to 1 hour.
Tread:	Mix of wide, grassy trail and hard-packed singletrack.
Aerobic level:	Moderate to strenuous.
Technical difficulty:	Levels 2 to 3+.
Hazards:	Exposed roots and loose rocks (often hidden in higher grass); wet, muddy areas.
Highlights:	Great sections of winding singletrack; unique slickrock riding on top of mountain; scenery too gorgeous for words.
Land status:	Superior National Forest.
Maps:	USGS Grand Marais; national forest maps; maps at trailhead.
Access:	From the Gunflint Trail (CR 12), follow County Road 53 and a sign for Pincushion trails to parking area. Trail starts on north side of the lot.

Notes on the trail: This is another cross-country ski trail system, but it is much more bike-friendly than many of the previous ski loops. Most sections of this area have well-defined dirt singletrack, and the grass isn't high enough to hide potential endo-causing impediments. There are a few wet stretches to deal with, but overall this is a great place to ride. A variety of difficulty levels makes these trails ideal for most enthusiasts; however, even the easiest ones require that riders be in shape.

The North Advanced Loop lives up to its name, with plenty of steep climbs and descents and sharp turns over fairly technical terrain. The highlight, of course, is Pincushion Mountain itself, bald on top with scattered tufts of dwarf pine and other foliage. A short hike from the outer edge of the main loop takes you up to the top, and once there you can ride along the northern part, getting a little taste of slickrock riding made famous in Moab, Utah. I'm begging you, do this ride in the fall to get the full effect of the view from up here. If you didn't know where you were, you'd swear Lake Superior was an ocean out there. On a clear day, you can

An epic view from Pincushion Mountain along the North Shore.

see the Apostle Islands nearly 100 miles away on the Wisconsin shore. Incredible. Head up here, pull up a piece of rock, and sit for a spell. Close your eyes; take a deep breath. How cool is this place?

The Ride

0.0 Ride past the trailhead kiosk and into the woods. Trail starts right off with a groovy little descent on dirt singletrack. Go straight ahead at your first junction (4), following the sign for Pincushion Mountain Loop. Trails out here are very well-marked with a sign at each junction, so there's little worry about getting lost, and you don't need to fumble with a map to find your way.

0.42 Take the right fork. There are some wet spots through this section, but otherwise trail is in great shape.

0.94 Junction 7 take a right.

1.9 Pass by the Superior Hiking Trail. Bikes aren't allowed on that trail, so stay away.

2.3 Junction with access trail to the top of the mountain. Hike your bike up the path and then up a steep rock face to reach the top.

Pincushion Mountain Trails

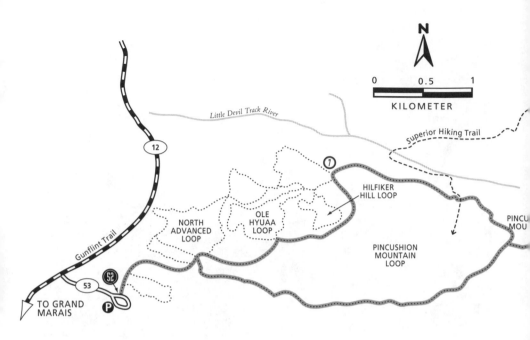

Once you get up, it's pretty fun to ride around on the exposed rock (but watch out for big, wheel-swallowing cracks). Head toward the north end and find a nice spot to soak in the incredible view of Lake Superior.

4.2 Head left here at Junction 4, back toward the trailhead.

4.6 Back at trailhead.

Note on riding up in these parts: The experts at Superior North Outdoor Center in Grand Marais will remind you that much of the riding around here is "adventure mountain biking." There are thousands of miles of roads, logging paths, and trails out in these woods, and many of them are unmarked and unmapped. Mark from SNOC told me he's been riding up here for more than fifteen years and just the other day found a trail he had never been on before. You can easily spend a week here exploring, and you can also very easily get hopelessly lost and be left for dead if you're not prepared. Pack along repair tools and first aid, and bring plenty of food and water, and for crying out loud, bring a compass and know how to use it. If you're desperate, follow a creek or river and you'll probably find Lake Superior. Best bet: stop in at Superior North for expert guidance. They've got good maps of the area, a full-service shop, and even offer guided lodge-to-lodge bike vacations.

Devil Track Lake Loop

Location:	11 miles northwest of Grand Marais on Cook County Road 57.
Distance:	24.2-mile loop.
Time:	3–4 hours.
Tread:	Gravel forest road; paved and gravel county road; grassy trail.
Aerobic level:	Easy to moderate.
Technical difficulty:	Levels 2 to 3.
Hazards:	Hidden obstacles (roots, rocks, etc.) on trail portion; occasional vehicle traffic.
Highlights:	Quiet and scenic forest roads; remote trail riding; excellent camping nearby.
Land status:	Superior National Forest; Cook County.
Maps:	USGS Devil Track Lake; national forest maps; check with Mark at Adventure North in Grand Marais for detailed info.
Access:	This loop starts from Devil Track Lake Campground. The campground is located on CR 57. From Gunflint Trail, follow CR 8 to CR 57, then west to campground.

Notes on the trail: Long miles of forest road await in the Superior National Forest, and this loop offers 25 of them with a mix of scenic road riding and a remote trail. The distance is long for a mountain bike ride, and the section through the woods on the North Shore State Trail rattles your bones pretty good. Several options exist here to change gears a bit if you want: Just ride the trail portion as an out-and-back ride, stay on the western forest roads for scenic cruising, or stay closer to "civilization" on the county roads to the east. The state trail is a very beautiful ride, but the grass is high enough to hide the roots and rocks and holes that make the ride a little taxing. Also, stay alert to the different hunting seasons to avoid taking a bullet, or at least wear your blaze-orange lycra. The campground at Devil Track Lake is a good one, and a fine place to establish your base camp.

Devil Track Lake Loop

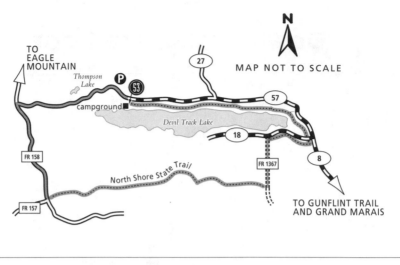

The Ride

0.0 Ride west from the campground on CR 57, a smooth gravel road with a couple of rollers along the way.

1.1 Pass scenic Thompson Lake on the right. This is an ideal ride in the fall of the year with the thick woods on both sides of the road.

3.1 Junction with Bally Creek Road (also known as Forest Road 158); go left. A short side trip north (right) on FR 158 will take you to the trailhead for Eagle Mountain, the highest point in Minnesota at 2,301 feet. The north fork of the Cascade River flows to your right as you ride south. Once again, multiple spur roads and trails branch off the main road, beckoning to be explored.

6.1 Junction with North Shore State Trail; turn left onto the wide, grassy path. Prepare for a bumpy ride all the way through. This is a pretty remote section and very quiet. Look for moose, deer, and Bigfoot.

14.7 Junction with Forest Road 1367; go left on the unimproved road to County Road 18, then right (east) to County Road 8.

17.5 Junction with CR 8; go left and follow this road back to CR 57 and the campground.

24.2 Back at trailhead.

54

Pike Lake Loop

Location:	Approximately 4 miles northwest of Cascade River State Park and MN Highway 61.
Distance:	17-mile loop (option to ride another section of state trail).
Time:	1.5–2 hours.
Tread:	Smooth gravel road to rustic logging road/trail.
Aerobic level:	Moderate + (strenuous if you consider the distance).
Technical difficulty:	Levels 2 to 3.
Hazards:	Big rocks; loose rocks and deep gravel; exposed roots and erosion gullies.
Highlights:	Excellent views of high ridgelines; fun riding on skinny logging path; very remote.
Land status:	Superior National Forest.
Maps:	USGS Mark Lake; national forest maps; Superior Mountain Bike Trail maps.
Access:	Best place to start is at the junction of County Road 45 and Forest Road 332. Ride west on the narrow gravel road.

Notes on the trail: This loop offers some great riding, with great views to match. Right off the bat you can check out splendid fall colors on two high ridgelines adjacent to Deer Yard Lake. Soon after that, the trail morphs into a skinny trail hugging the edge of Pike Lake, with fun boulders to ride over or around. The North Shore State Trail passes through the middle of this loop and allows for an optional shortcut or more miles of trail riding. (I recommend this choice. The state trail sneaks between some higher ridges and has nice views of Pike Lake.) Of course, if you're into big miles, these roads connect to a half-dozen others to form multiple loop options to potentially keep you riding all week.

The Ride

0.0 Begin riding west from CR 45 on Forest Road 332. Just over a half-mile in, you'll meet the junction with a spur trail that leads down to Deer Yard Lake.

Pike Lake Loop

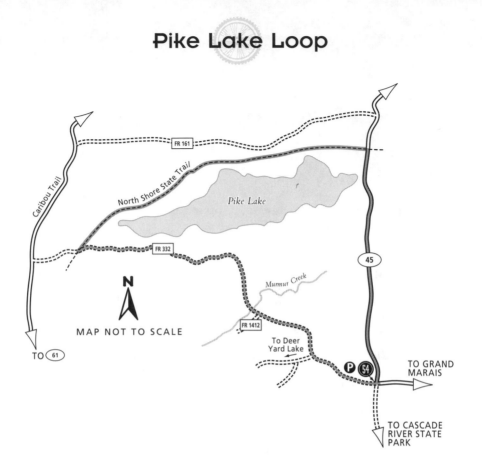

1.3   Junction with Forest Road 1412 and two other spur trails, all of which offer more cool places to ride. FR 1412 will lead you down toward Caribou Lake. Our path curves hard right here and crosses over Murmur Creek.

2.2   FR 332 branches to the left here, while another gated trail goes right. Obviously, we'll go left. Now the road becomes more of a trail: narrow with big rocks and encroaching shrubbery on both sides.

5.4   Trail kisses the west shore of Pike Lake, then turns back into a maintained forest road.

6.9   Junction with the North Shore State Trail; turn right into the woods. (For 10 extra miles, continue straight here to Caribou Trail and head north to FR 161. Follow FR 161 east to CR 45, and south to trailhead.) The trail skirts around a small mountain and climbs up to about 1,700 feet. Great views all around as you gradually drop back down.

15.1   Junction with CR 45; go right.

17.0   Back at trailhead.

Pancore Lake Loop

Location:	13 miles north of Tofte on MN Highway 61 on the Sawbill Trail.
Distance:	19.8-mile loop.
Time:	2.5–3 hours.
Tread:	Gravel road and primitive forest road.
Aerobic level:	Moderate.
Technical difficulty:	Levels 2 to 3.
Hazards:	Some loose gravel; larger rocks in trail; some vehicle traffic.
Highlights:	Secluded ride along scenic rivers; lake access and campgrounds nearby; several other loops in the area.
Land status:	Superior National Forest; private.
Maps:	USGS Mark Lake; national forest maps.
Access:	Several starting points available, but this loop begins at junction of Sawbill Trail (County Road 2) and Forest Road 338. Start here and head northeast on the narrow forest road.

Notes on the trail: This is another long loop that combines primitive and maintained forest road riding in a remote setting. In the fall, you get the bonus of riding among the fall colors and alongside the picturesque Temperance and Poplar Rivers. Again, you're unlikely to see a soul out here, except maybe a car on the Sawbill. Trail conditions vary from smooth gravel to rough rock and dirt. If the season is right, there are blueberry patches en route for an extra treat. Also, two other large loop clusters are close by for added variety.

The Ride

0.0 From the Sawbill Trail (County Road 2), start riding northeast on the narrow FR 338. At about 2.5 miles in you'll pass a carry-in access path for Pancore Lake.

3.0 You should start to see glimpses of the Poplar River off to your left.

Pancore Lake Loop

MAP NOT TO SCALE

4.9 Junction with Forest Road 340; go left and then left again on Forest Road 339. Follow this all the way to . . .

10.3 Junction with Forest Road 170; turn left. This is a gravel forest road; it almost immediately crosses over the Temperance River.

12.2 Junction with the Sawbill Trail (CR 2); go left and head south back to the trailhead.

19.8 Back at trailhead and FR 338.

Ninemile Lake Loop

Location: 11.5 miles northeast of Finland on County Road 7.

Distance: 20.3-mile loop

Time: 2.5–3.5 hours.

Tread: Mix of loose and hard-packed gravel road.

Aerobic level: Easy +.

Technical difficulty: Levels 1 to 2.

Hazards: Big gravel trucks at warp speed; some loose gravel.

Highlights: Very remote and quiet; easy riding through dense woods of two different forests.

Land status: Finland State Forest and Superior National Forest.

Maps: USGS Finland; USFS Superior National Forest.

Access: From MN Highway 61, head northwest on MN Highway 1 for 6.4 miles to the burg of Finland. Turn right on CR 7; the pavement ends after 1 mile. Follow CR 7 for 10 more miles to the junction with County Road 8. I used this spot as a trailhead, but feel free to start back in Finland if you really want to pile on the miles.

Notes on the trail: This is a great ride for finding plenty of peace and quiet while meandering along remote forest roads. It got to be an endurance quest toward the end, but this loop serves up some first-rate northwoods riding. There are several doubletrack trails branching off the main road that could be fun to explore, and picturesque Ninemile and Hare Lakes make an ideal rest stop. The monster gravel trucks coming hell-bent right at me were a little unnerving, but overall there was very little traffic. If you're super fit, you might start this ride in Finland for a 40-mile marathon tour. Either way, this is a fairly isolated area with next to nothing around (including help if you decide to get yourself injured). Be prepared with plenty of food and water and first aid—and bring a compass.

Ninemile Lake Loop

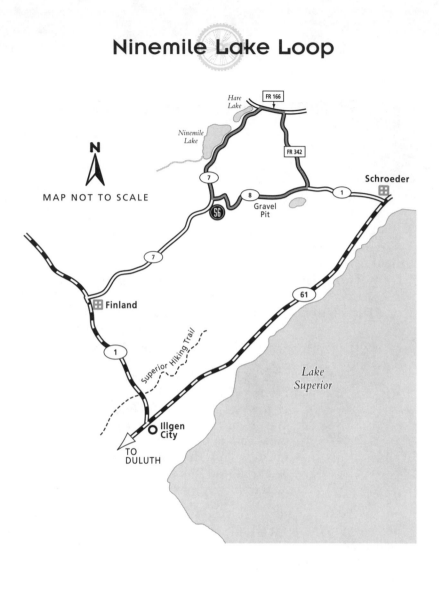

Hare
Lake

FR 166

Ninemile
Lake

FR 342

N

MAP NOT TO SCALE

7

8

Gravel
Pit

56

1

Schroeder

7

61

Finland

1

Lake
Superior

Superior Hiking Trail

Illgen
City

TO
DULUTH

The Ride

0.0 From the junction of CR 7 and CR 8, ride east (toward Lake Superior), following signs for the town of Schroeder. The road is rolling with some washboard sections and heavy truck traffic. You will

Great fall riding on the Ninemile Lake Loop, Superior National Forest.

eventually pass the gravel pit, and the trucks go away after that.

4.3 Road morphs into County Road 1; continue straight ahead.

6.4 Go left on Forest Road 342. Enjoy a beautiful rolling ride for several miles.

11.6 Junction with Forest Road 166; go left.

13.6 Junction with CR 7; go left, paralleling Hare Lake and Ninemile Lake on your right. Lots of fine places along here to stop and replenish your fuel tank.

20.3 Back at trailhead and junction with CR 8.

Katherine Lake Trail

Location:	Ride starts in Finland, 6.5 miles northwest of Illgen City and MN Highway 61.
Distance:	34 miles out and back with options for shorter mileage.
Time:	3+ hours.
Tread:	Mix of hard-packed and loose gravel road.
Aerobic level:	Easy+.
Technical difficulty:	Level 2.
Hazards:	Some loose gravel; traffic going way too fast.
Highlights:	Quiet with good chances to spot wildlife; scenic Katherine Lake is a welcome sight after the long ride in.
Land status:	Superior National Forest; private.
Maps:	USGS Silver Bay; USFS Superior National Forest.
Access:	Park in an out-of-the-way place in downtown Finland and ride west on Heffelfinger Forest Road.

Notes on the trail: This trail is another sample of some nontechnical forest road riding in a relatively remote setting. There was a surprising amount of traffic when I was here, but it wasn't bad enough to ruin the day. The road isn't in as good condition as the previous ride, and it's not as scenic until you near Katherine Lake, but it's still enjoyable to be out there, just you and your bike. If you venture off the main road during hunting season, make sure you wear blaze orange and don't get stung by bird shot or a deer rifle. This is another long haul; consider starting farther along the road if you're not up for the mileage. Our Place tavern in Finland is a great place for a post-ride beverage.

The Ride

0.0   Start at junction of MN Highway 1 and Heffelfinger Forest Road; ride west on the paved road and continue on when it turns to gravel.

Katherine Lake Trail

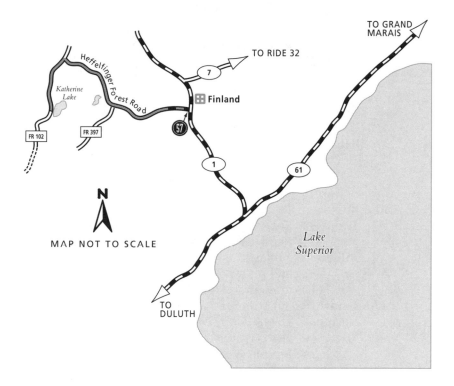

5.4   Pass junction with Beaver River Road (Forest Road 397).
13.2   Junction with Forest Road 102; go left.
17.0   Rest stop at Katherine Lake. Refuel and turn around.
34.0   Back at trailhead and Finland. Whew!

Hogback Lake Trail

Location:	Approximately 13 miles northwest of Schroeder and MN Highway 61.
Distance:	13-mile one-way trail.
Time:	1.5 hours.
Tread:	Smooth gravel forest road.
Aerobic level:	Easy+.
Technical difficulty:	Level 1+.
Hazards:	Vehicle traffic (heavier on weekends); some loose gravel or rocks on road.
Highlights:	Fantastic scenery; numerous lakes with access and picnic areas; big geologic moment as you cross the Laurentian Divide.
Land status:	Superior National Forest.
Maps:	USGS Cabin Lake; national forest maps.
Access:	Take County Road 1 west from Schroeder to Forest Road 342. Head north to Forest Road 166 west to County Road 7. Follow CR 7 to trailhead. Start this ride at Hogback Lake at junction of CR 7 and Forest Road 172.

Notes on the trail: I did this trail one-way from Hogback Lake to Isabella. It's a great ride on an excellent road, and the sights along the way are fabulous. A cluster of lakes halfway through provide a nice diversion (or even a chance to cool off), and it's worth stopping at the Laurentian Divide marker to learn some cool geologic stuff. The Divide separates watersheds flowing north to the Arctic Ocean and east to the Atlantic. It also splits a third time, directing more water south to the Gulf of Mexico. The ridge along this road is a couple of *billion* years old. After passing the Divide, the trail rolls up and down gently and deposits you on MN Highway 1 at Isabella. There are four or five spur trails and roads along the route (as usual) that can take you to more isolated parts of the forest.

The Ride

0.0 Ride west from Hogback Lake on FR 172. The road is in great shape, and passes scenic lakes and streams for the first few miles.

Hogback Lake Trail

6.3 Pass junction with Forest Road 362 on your left, then Forest Road 174 on the right.

8.0 Pass over the Laurentian Divide. This is a fun place for a rest stop.

11.6 Junction with Forest Road 369. This road leads to lake homes to the north, and there is typically more vehicle traffic here.

13.0 Junction with MN 1 and Isabella. Stop here or retrace your tracks for a long day of riding.

McDougal Lakes Trail

Location:	10 miles west of Isabella on MN Highway 1.
Distance:	14.3-mile loop.
Time:	1–1.5 hours.
Tread:	Gravel and primitive forest road and paved highway.
Aerobic level:	Moderate.
Technical difficulty:	Levels 1 to 2+.
Hazards:	Some loose rocks on road.
Highlights:	Fun loop on quiet trail; mix of rolling and flat terrain.
Land status:	Superior National Forest.
Maps:	USGS Isabella Station; national forest maps.
Access:	Ride north at the junction of MN 1 and Forest Road 383.

Notes on the trail: This little loop keeps you on your toes and is fun, with several changes in tread type. The route starts on tame gravel road, then gradually narrows to a more primitive path, and at the end there's even pavement! It doesn't take long to delve deep into the woods, and there were several herds of deer when I went through. A couple of spur trails offer expanded mileage, and the back half of the loop has a few steeper rollers to give you a light taste of climbing. The return trip on MN 1 is smooth as silk, but watch for traffic. McDougal Lakes Campground is close by for some scenic northwoods camping.

The Ride

0.0 Ride north from MN 1 on FR 383 (Bandana Lake Road). It starts out as a smooth gravel road, then turns a little rockier with a couple of small, rolling hills.

3.4 Pass a narrow doubletrack trail on your left. This trail actually goes through and meets with the back side of this loop if you're looking for a shortcut.

5.9 T intersection with Forest Road 386; go left.

McDougal Lakes Trail

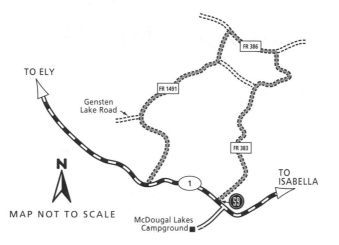

TO ELY

Gensten Lake Road

FR 386

FR 1491

FR 383

N

TO ISABELLA

MAP NOT TO SCALE

1

59

McDougal Lakes Campground ■

6.8   Junction with Forest Road 1491; turn left. Gorgeous stretch of trail with a soft carpet of pine needles and leaves, and scattered boulders to liven things up.

7.6   Pass spur trail coming in from the left.

8.9   Junction with Gensten Lake Road; keep going straight ahead.

12.9   Junction with MN 1; turn left and head back to the trailhead.

14.3   Back at trailhead.

Note to road riders: MN 1 between Isabella and Ely is one of the most beautiful pieces of road I've ever been on. It rolls and twists and turns for more than 50 miles on pavement that's smooth as a baby's bottom. In many places there is little to no shoulder, so that's one drawback, and there can be a bit of traffic on weekends, but those are minor inconveniences. This is a slice of Heaven, my friends.

Grassy Lake Trail

The next two rides highlight some forest road riding opportunities at the north end of the unofficial system of mountain bike rides in the Ely area. McDougal Lakes and the Kawishiwi area make up the southern section.

Location:	13 miles north of Ely on the Echo Trail.
Distance:	8.7 miles out and back.
Time:	1 hour and change.
Tread:	Maintained and primitive forest road.
Aerobic level:	Easy +.
Technical difficulty:	Levels 1 to 2.
Hazards:	Some loose gravel and rocks on trail.
Highlights:	Very quiet; entry point to Boundary Waters Canoe Area (BWCA); excellent campground nearby; good beginner ride.
Land status:	Superior National Forest.
Maps:	USGS Shagawa Lake; national forest maps.
Access:	Start at junction of Echo Trail and Forest Road 459. Ride east on the wide gravel road.

Notes on the trail: This is a nice little trail that gives you another taste of great autumn colors; maple, aspen, and sumac mix with pine along the route and on the shores of adjacent lakes. The end of the main road allows access to the Boundary Waters. Fenske Lake Campground extends all of the best qualities of the northwoods. It's a beautiful place with huge white pines and several stunning campsites on the shores of Fenske Lake. I was fortunate enough to hear the ghostly howls of a large pack of timber wolves the night I was there. Speaking of wolves, be sure to visit the International Wolf Center in Ely for everything you always wanted to know about those beasts and get permits and details for the BWCA and adjacent lands.

The Ride

0.0 Ride northeast from Echo Trail on the wide gravel FR 459. Some bigger bumps and rocks along the way, and a couple of small hills.

3.5 Turn right at road for Grassy Lake public access. Continuing

Grassy Lake Trail, Lonesome Lake Trail

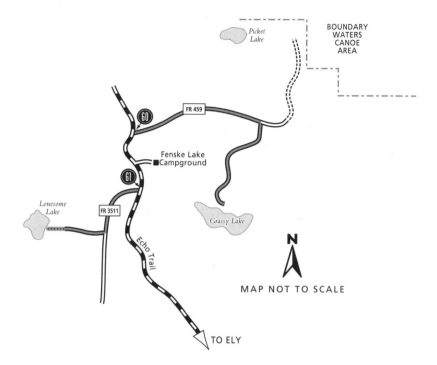

Picket
Lake

BOUNDARY
WATERS
CANOE
AREA

FR 459

60

Fenske Lake
■Campground

61

Lonesome
Lake

FR 3511

Grassy Lake

Echo Trail

N

MAP NOT TO SCALE

TO ELY

straight here will deliver you to Picket Lake and entry to the BWCA.

4.4 Grassy Lake road dead-ends here. A narrow footpath wanders off into the woods and down to the lake. You can ride it for a short way, then it gets too overgrown.

8.7 Back at trailhead at Echo Trail. A short ride south on "the Echo" will take you right to the next ride to Lonesome Lake.

Lonesome Lake Trail

See map on page 167.

Location:	12 miles north of Ely on the Echo Trail.
Distance:	3.6 miles out and back.
Time:	30–45 minutes.
Tread:	Gravel forest road and a short piece of single-track.
Aerobic level:	Easy +.
Technical difficulty:	Level 1 +.
Hazards:	None.
Highlights:	Great ride in dense woods with no one around; secluded, scenic lake for quality time with nature.
Land status:	Superior National Forest.
Maps:	USGS Shagawa Lake; national forest maps.
Access:	I started this ride at the entrance to Fenske Lake Campground. You can also start right at Echo Trail and Forest Road 3511, 0.25 mile south of the campground.

Notes on the trail: This is a really fun ride on excellent roads. The "trail" sends you up and down some small hills as it winds through thick woods, with more of those hulking red and white pines to lead the way. There is also a bevy of maple and aspen that blaze bright in the fall and spoil your concentration. A fun (but very short) singletrack trail leads down to a quiet lake that isn't on many maps and isn't named—I dubbed it Lonesome Lake. There's a nice spot by the shore to set down and absorb the peace of the place, especially around dawn on a crisp autumn morning. Keep your eyes open for moose. Also, check out the great hiking trail to Bass Lake just down the road a piece

The Ride

0.0 From Fenske Lake Campground, ride south for 0.25 mile to FR 3511. Turn right onto the narrow gravel road. A fairly steep climb with deeper gravel presents a brief challenge about a half-mile in.

1.8 Junction with public water access to Lonesome Lake. Follow the footpath on the right down to the lake for a view of a consummate North Country scene. Linger awhile, then retrace your tracks back to the Echo Trail. FR 3511 also continues south from here toward Everett Lake and Twin Lakes for a longer ride.

3.6 Back at Echo Trail. Turn left and ride 0.25 mile up to the campground for a 3.8-mile ride.

Hidden Valley Ski Trails

Location:	On the eastern fringe of Ely, adjacent to the International Wolf Center.
Distance:	15 miles of trails available.
Time:	45 minutes to all day.
Tread:	Grassy ski trails.
Aerobic level:	Moderate to strenuous.
Technical difficulty:	Levels 2 to 4 (for steep climbs).
Hazards:	Grassy tread hides obstacles; potential crashes on steep descents.
Highlights:	Very scenic; great views from the old ski jump area; multiple loops to choose from; easy access to a flat ride around Shagawa Lake.
Land status:	Superior National Forest; City of Ely.
Maps:	USGS Ely; maps from Ely Nordic Association and area outfitters.
Access:	Start from the upper parking lot of the chalet area at the retired ski jump. Choose from four different trails.

Notes on the trail: Hidden Valley offers some pretty good riding for a ski area. The views of Ely and the Superior National Forest are tremendous and plentiful from the high hills, especially right at the base of the old ski jump. The riding is typically tougher in the high grass, but the trails are well-maintained, and there are plenty of challenging hills to test your climbing and descending skills. The one thing that's missing is a good map of the place; I had a tough time finding the less-than-adequate one in this book. But the trails all loop around back to the trailhead, so it's a fun place to run around in.

The Ride

From the parking area, pick a trail and head out. The gravel road past the gate will take you right up to the ski jump and some super views of the surrounding area. You can access other loops from there, or start from the bottom and pick your favorite. The trails in the lower valley tend to be wet more often than not. Past the powerline there are some big hills to climb,

Hidden Valley Ski Trails

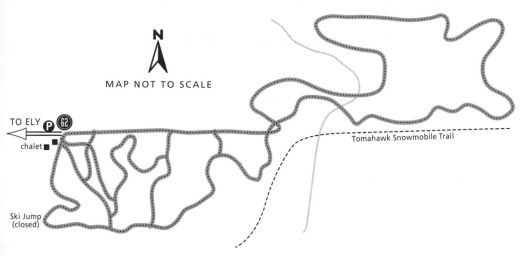

MAP NOT TO SCALE

N

TO ELY

chalet

62

Tomahawk Snowmobile Trail

Ski Jump
(closed)

but you'll get plenty of downhill action, too. A short ride down Hidden Valley Road (the access to the ski jump) will take you to the Wolf Center and MN Highway 169. You can cross there onto a paved path that connects with the Trezona Trail for a relaxed cruise around Shagawa Lake. There is also access to the Taconite State Trail from MN Highway 1 in Ely.

Kawishiwi River Trail

Location:	15 miles south of Ely on MN Highway 1.
Distance:	11.9-miles out and back.
Time:	1–1.5 hours.
Tread:	Maintained and primitive forest road.
Aerobic level:	Easy to moderate.
Technical difficulty:	Levels 1 to 2.
Hazards:	Some vehicle traffic; large rocks in road; easy to get lost on spur trails.
Highlights:	Fun ride on scenic road and narrow forest trail; access to Boundary Waters Canoe Area (BWCA); several spur trails for additional loops.
Land status:	Superior National Forest.
Maps:	USGS Slate Lake East; national forest maps.
Access:	Start at MN 1 and Forest Road 181 (Spruce Road). Ride northeast on the wide gravel road.

Narrow forest road at edge of the BWCA-Kawishiwi River Trail.

Kawishiwi River Trail

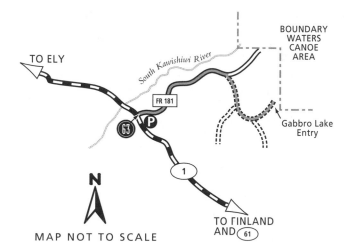

MAP NOT TO SCALE

Notes on the trail: This is a great ride with a mix of forest road and forest trails. FR 181 is a major entry point to the BWCA, so you might see a car or three on the way, but it's generally very quiet. Once you split from the road, the fun really begins as the trail turns to skinny doubletrack and reaches deeper into the forest. Two or three spur trails show themselves on the way down to Omaday Lake, inviting you in. The Tomahawk Snowmobile Trail also winds through this area, providing yet another option for a side trip. This is another excellent fall color ride.

The Ride

0.0   From MN 1, ride northeast on FR 181.

3.8   Pass the South Kawishiwi River entry point to the BWCA.

4.8   Road forks. Main road continues to the Gabbro Lake entry point; we'll go straight here onto the narrow doubletrack trail. Some loose rocks in the road, but no other hazards to worry about.

5.9   I turned around here at the edge of one of the flowages from Gabbro Lake. You could also start from the Gabbro cut-off from the main road, or even park in by the gravel pit and just explore these fun trails.

11.9 Back at MN 1.

Appendix A

More Fun Rides

FRENCH RAPIDS TRAILS

More than 10 miles of trails along the Mississippi River near Brainerd. Choose from a half-dozen loops on this cross-country ski system. Plenty of good ups and downs, rolling through a mixed forest setting.

TIMBER/WHITEFISH LAKE AREA

Close to 50 miles of relatively tame forest roads and rustic logging roads northwest of Tofte. Check area ranger stations for maps and route suggestions.

MYRE-BIG ISLAND STATE PARK

Some 7 miles of trails way down at the southern border of our state, a short spin southeast of Albert Lea. Gently rolling terrain (with a couple of longer climbs) in a prairie landscape with wildlife aplenty. Nice campground in park with easy access from I-35.

STATE TRAILS

Try one of the fifteen DNR State Trails for long and scenic rides. Here are the top ten:

Root River: 42-mile paved trail from Fountain to Houston in southeast Minnesota. One of the prettiest rides in the state.

Sakatah Singing Hills: Thirty-nine miles of paved trail between Mankato and Faribault. Another relaxing cruise. Nice bluffland scenery near Kato.

Luce Line: A 63-mile excursion if you do the whole thing. Crushed limestone surface with some natural and paved segments. Several trailheads available.

Gateway: Excellent paved starting near downtown St. Paul and finishing up in Stillwater. Heavily used on summer weekends.

Willard Munger: Mix in some road riding and take this trail all the way to Duluth. Natural surface trail on Boundary Segment (through St. Croix State Park); great paved riding from Hinkley to Duluth. Part of the annual MS 150 ride.

Paul Bunyan: Another monster (over 100 miles) stretching from Brainerd to Bemidji. Beautiful riding through grandeur of the northwoods.

Heartland: This one crosses right over Mr. Bunyan's trail and takes you through the Chippewa National Forest to gorgeous lake country.

Taconite: Four paved miles and 159 miles of snowmobile trail. That oughta fill up most of a weekend.

Arrowhead: Start in Tower and ride to Canada! There are only about 69 miles of decent trail for riding; the rest of the trail is riddled with wet spots.

North Shore: An epic natural-surface trail following the Sawtooth Mountains and the shore of Lake Superior up to Grand Marais. Best riding is from Finland north— about 75 miles of trail.

Appendix B

Information Sources

The Minnesota Department of Natural Resources and our two national forests offer a wealth of information on state parks and state forests. Their offices are also the best places to go for current trail status (conditions, access, open/closed, etc.). Also check regional offices, and the

DNR Info Center
Box 40, 500 Lafayette Road
St. Paul, MN 55155
(651) 296–6157
(800) 766–6000
State Parks & Recreation (651) 296–9223
Trails & Waterways (651) 297–1151
www.dnr.state.mn.us

STATE FOREST CONTACT INFORMATION

Contact officials at these locations for current trail status. (Not all state forest areas are listed.)

Bemidji Area
Area Forester
2220 Bemidji Avenue
Bemidji, MN 56601
(218) 755–2890

Blackduck Area
Area Forester
HC3 95B
Blackduck, MN 56630
(218) 835–6684

Park Rapids Area
Area Forester
Box 113 – 607 W. First Street
Park Rapids, MN 56470
(218) 732–3309

Effie Area
Area Forester
Box 95
Deer River Area
Area Forester
Box 157
Deer River, MN 56636
(218) 246–8343

Two Harbors Area
Area Forester
1568 Highway 2
Two Harbors, MN 55616
(218) 834–6600

Brainerd Area
Area Forester
1601 Minnesota Drive
Braincrd, MN 56401
(218) 828–2565

Tower Area
Area Forester
Tower, MN 55790
(218) 753-4500

Backus Area
Area Forester
Box 6
Backus, MN 56435
(218) 947-3232

Lewiston Area
Area Forester
Box 279
Lewiston, MN 55952
(507) 523-2183

STATE PARK CONTACT INFORMATION

Afton
Hastings
(651) 436-5391

Gooseberry Falls
Two Harbors
(218) 834-3855

Jay Cooke
Carlton
(218) 384-4610

Lake Bemidji
Bemidji
(218) 755-3843

McCarthy Beach
Side Lake
(218) 254-2411

MN Valley Rec. Area
Jordan
(612) 492-6400

Scenic
Bigfork
(218) 743-3362

Savanna Portage
McGregor
(218) 426-3271

St. Croix
Hinkley
(320) 384-6591

Split Rock Lighthouse
Two Harbors
(218) 226-6377

COUNTY PARKS – METRO AREA

Ramsey County Parks &
Recreation
2015 Van Dyke Street
Maplewood, MN 55109
(651) 748-2500

Hennepin County Parks
12615 County Road 9
Plymouth, MN 55441
(612) 559-9000

Washington County Parks
1515 Keats Avenue N.
Lake Elmo, MN 55042
(651) 731-3851

Dakota County Parks
8500 127th Street E.
Hastings, MN 55033
(651) 438-4660

City of St. Paul Parks & Recreation
25 W. 4th Street, #300
St. Paul, MN 55102
(651) 266-6400

City of Burnsville Parks & Recreation
100 Civic Center Parkway
Burnsville, MN 55337

Minnesota Valley National Wildlife Refuge
3815 E. 80th Street
Bloomington, MN 55425
(612) 335-2323

SUPERIOR NATIONAL FOREST

Supervisor's Office
8901 Grand Avenue Place
Duluth, MN 55808
(218) 626-4300

Gunflint Ranger District
P.O. Box 790
Grand Marais, MN 55604
(218) 387-1750

Kawishiwi Ranger District
118 S. 4th Avenue E.
Ely, MN 55731
(218) 365-7600

LaCroix Ranger District
320 N. Highway 53
Cook, MN 55723
(218) 666-0020

Laurentian Ranger District
318 Forestry Road
Aurora, MN 55705
(218) 229-8800

Tofte Ranger District
Tofte, MN 55615
(218) 663-7280

CHIPPEWA NATIONAL FOREST

Supervisor's Office
Route 3, Box 244
Cass Lake, MN 56633
(218) 335-8600

Blackduck Ranger District
HC 3, Box 95
Blackduck, MN 56630
(218) 835-4291

Cass Lake Ranger District
Route 3, Box 219
Cass Lake, MN 56633
(218) 335-8600

Deer River Ranger District
P.O. Box 308
Deer River, MN 56636
(218) 246-2123

Marcell Ranger District
HC1, Box 15
Marcell, MN 56657
(218) 832-3161

Walker Ranger District
73, Box 15
Walker, MN 56484
(218) 547-1044

A Short Index of Rides

This index lists seven different prominent features of area rides. Most rides appear somewhere in this index (some more than once) to allow you to associate a particular trip with what you can expect on the trail.

Glossary

ATB: All-terrain bicycle; a.k.a. mountain bike, fat tire flier, dirt dog.

ATV: All-terrain vehicle; in this book ATV refers to off-road motorcycles and four-wheelers.

Bail: Getting off the bike, usually in a hurry, and many times not by choice. Often a last resort. Also a verb indicating a course of action: "Let's bail after we finish this last climb."

Bunny hop: Leaping up, while riding, lifting both wheels off the ground to jump over an obstacle (or just for the fun of it).

Clean: To ride without touching a foot (or other body part) to the ground; to ride a tough section successfully.

Clipless: A type of pedal with a binding mechanism that accepts a special cleat on the soles of bike shoes. These pedals offer more power and control, especially when climbing, and (usually) release your foot in a crash.

Contour: A line on a topographic map showing a continuous elevation level over uneven ground. Also a verb indicating a fairly easy or moderate grade: "The trail contours around the western fringe of the ridge."

Downfall: Trees or branches that have fallen across the trail.

Doubletrack: A trail, jeep road, ATV route, or other track with two distinct ribbons of **tread**, typically with grass growing in between. No matter which side you choose, the other rut always looks smoother. Also used to describe a trail wider than singletrack but narrower than a road.

Endo: Lifting the rear wheel off the ground and riding (or abruptly not riding) on the front wheel only. Also known, at various degrees of control and finality, as a nose wheelie, "going over the bars," and a faceplant. No matter what it's called, it usually hurts.

Faceplant: See **Endo.**

Fall line: The angle and direction of a slope; the **line** you follow when gravity is in control and you aren't.

Granny gear: The lowest (easiest) gear on your bike. Typically, this gear choice has you spinning the pedals like crazy while making slow but consistent progress. On the really steep stuff, you'll be thanking your granny for that low gear.

Hammer: To ride hard; derived from how it feels afterward: "I'm hammered."

2462

Hammerhead: Someone who actually enjoys feeling **hammered.** A Type A rider who goes hard and fast all the time.

Header: See **Endo.**

Line: The route (or trajectory) between or over obstacles or through turns. **Tread** or trail refers to the ground you're riding on; the line is the path you choose within the tread (and may only exist in your imagination).

Out-of-the-saddle: Riding with your butt off the saddle and really stomping on the pedals; commonly done during a sprint or a climb.

Quads: Thigh muscles (short for quadriceps); or maps in the USGS topographic series (short for quadrangles). The right quads (of either kind) can prevent or get you out of trouble in the north woods.

Singletrack: A trail, game run, or other track with only one ribbon of **tread.** A good piece of singletrack is pure fat tire fun.

Spur: A side road or trail that splits off from the main route.

Surf: Riding through loose gravel or sand, when the wheels slalom from side to side. Also *heavy surf*: frequent and difficult obstacles.

Suspension: Shock absorption. A bike with front suspension has a shock-absorbing fork or stem. Rear suspension absorbs shock between the rear wheel and frame. A bike with both is said to be fully suspended and rides like a Cadillac.

Switchback: A zigzag (or S-shaped) turn as the trail climbs up a steep slope. There are few "real" switchbacks in Minnesota due to our terrain's minimal elevation gain.

Track stand: Balancing on a bike in one place, without rolling forward appreciably. Cock the front wheel to one side and bring that pedal up to the 1 or 2 o'clock position. Now control your side-to-side balance by applying pressure on the pedals and brakes and changing the angle of the front wheel, as needed. It takes practice but really comes in handy at stoplights and when trying to free a foot from your pedal before falling.

Tread: The riding surface.

Water bar: A log, board, or other barrier placed in the trail to divert water off the trail and prevent erosion. Water bars have the potential to send you to the ground in a hurry, even when conditions are favorable.

About the Author

Steve Johnson is the author of two other FalconGuides, *Mountain Biking Chequamegon* and *Mountain Biking the Twin Cities*. He has also written for publications like *Bicycling, Hooked on the Outdoors,* and *Silent Sports.* A road racer at heart, he discovered a taste for dirt while attending college in the Colorado mountains. Steve currently lives with his wife in St. Paul.